Mexico

Mexico

Text by Don Allan
Revised by Wendy Luft
Photography: Mireille Vautier, pages 4, 5, 8, 10, 13, 17,
18, 21, 24-25, 28, 48-49, 52, 57, 61, 88, 94, 107, 113,
121, 130, 134, 141, 143, 151, 153, 154, 157, 167, 173,
174-175, 190, 192, 194, 196-197, 200, 202, 205, 208,
212, 217; Claude Huber, pages 41, 55, 64, 72, 84-85,
211; Adriano Heitmann, pages 32-33, 36-37, 66-67, 73,
77, 80, 93, 102, 104, 116-117, 122, 131, 145, 146, 162,
168, 179, 180, 183, 185, 189, 201, 218.
Cover photograph by Claude Huber
Photo Editor: Naomi Zinn
Research: Claudia Velo
Layout: Media Content Marketing, Inc.
Cartography by Ortelius Design

Thirteenth Edition 2002

CONTACTING THE EDITORS
Every effort has been made to provide accurate information in this publication, but
changes are inevitable. The publisher cannot be responsible for any resulting loss,
inconvenience or injury. We would appreciate it if readers would call our attention to
any errors or outdated information by contacting Berlitz Publishing, PO Box 7910,
London SE1 1WE, England. Fax: (44) 20 7403 0290;
e-mail: berlitz@apaguide.demon.co.uk

050/213 REV

CONTENTS

● A (☞) in the text denotes a highly recommended sight

Mexico

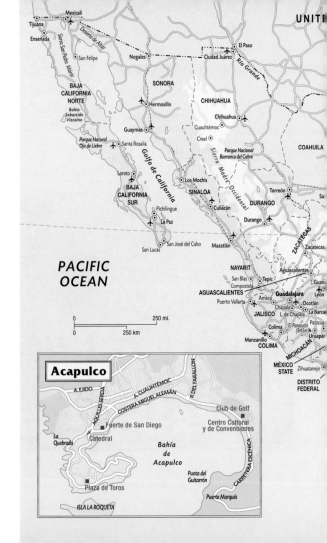

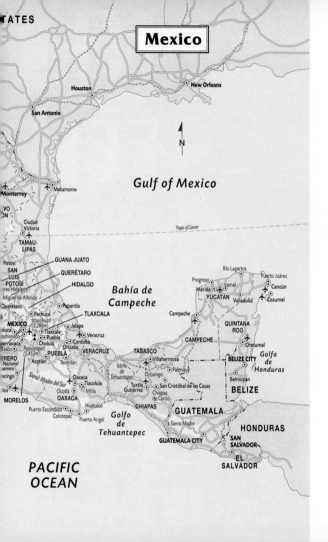

THE COUNTRY
AND ITS PEOPLE

In his personal account of the conquest of Mexico in 1519, Bernal Díaz del Castillo described the way he and his fellow Spaniards reacted when, from the slopes of the snow-capped volcano Popocatépetl, they beheld the valley of Mexico for the first time. Far below was a broad, fertile plain, many miles across, surrounded by steep mountains. Three lakes occupied the valley, with exotic cities on their fringes. Tenochtitlán, the most beautiful of all, lay in the middle of the largest lake, connected to the shore by three elevated causeways and the constant traffic of boats that plied back and forth from the coast. The city was larger than any Spanish city of the time; it had broad canals and brightly colored pyramids and palaces, with large, colorful banners fluttering in the air. So beautiful and strange was the scene that the Spaniards lacked anything with which to compare it except for the magical kingdoms that populated chivalric novels (the pulp fiction of their time) – a comparison that placed the Spaniards in the role of knights errant and created the possibility of encountering dragons and wizards.

The reaction of these Spaniards is something akin to what is still provoked in visitors to Mexico who come unprepared for the most exotic features of the land and its people, and who often refer to works of fiction when trying to communicate their Mexican experiences. Like the conquistadors, modern visitors note the vivid colors – from the warm reds, yellows, and oranges of contemporary Mexican architecture to the cool blues and greens of its seacoasts. Accentuating this brightly colored palette are the contrasts that Mexico presents. A short ride on horseback in Mexico can take the rider from the cool, thin fragrances of high-mountain pine forests to the warm, heady aromas of tropical jungle – never mind what a car ride can do. Walk into a bank, and you might be tended by an impeccably dressed man in a navy

You may just come across a clan such as this one while traveling down the road in Oaxaca and other rural areas in Mexico.

blue three-piece suit, while in line next to you stands a Zapotec Indian woman dressed in an equally impeccable, beautifully worked crimson *huipil* (Indian blouse). Anybody who travels to Mexico will find in the land and its inhabitants much to marvel at.

Mexico is roughly half the size of Western Europe. It has a lot of coastline, due in part to the two great peninsulas that act as bookends for the country: Baja California in the northwest and the Yucatán in the southeast. If you don't take into account these peninsulas, Mexico has the shape of a cornucopia – wide at its northern border, narrow as it curls to the south and east before it joins Guatemala. It is an extremely mountainous country, with two long mountain ranges known as the Sierra Madre that descend from the United States border down the east and west sides of the country and converge in the central part, in effect forming a large "V" that encompasses the majority of national territory. The large area between the ranges is desert in the north and predominantly high tableland in the south. At the bottom of the "V" and cupped by these mountains is the valley of Mexico that gave Bernal Díaz such a shock, and in which now sits Mexico City, the nation's capital. The area surrounding this and neighboring valleys is the highest part of the country. Mexico's four tallest mountains (which are all snow-capped volcanoes) can be found here. In Mexico, the climate of a particular place has more to do with its altitude than with its latitude.

The Sierra Madre Occidental is the western mountain range that follows the Pacific coast. Etched into the northern part of these mountains between the city of Chihuahua and the port of Los Mochis are several spectacular canyons known collectively as Copper Canyon. This is the home of the Tarahumara Indians. In the southern part of the Sierra Madre, sheltered in the valleys, are some of the colonial silver cities. Along the entire western edge of this mountain range lies a narrow coastal plain, except where in some places the Sierra Madre extends all the way to the shore to create mountain-fringed bays of great beauty, such as at Puerto Vallarta. On the Gulf coast side of Mexico runs the Sierra Madre Oriental. These mountains receive more rain and are greener than the western range. They have some lovely waterfalls and deep limestone caverns, and to their east is a broad coastal plain where lies most of the state of Veracruz, including the port city of the same name.

South and east of central Mexico are the Oaxacan highlands, home of the Zapotec and Mixtec Indians who live near Oaxaca City and are famous for their many handcrafts. Mexico gets much narrower as the Pacific coast bends eastwards. There is another mountain range, the Sierra Madre del Sur, that follows this coast, making it almost entirely mountainous. Here you find beach resorts like Acapulco, with its famous cliffs, and Ixtapa/Zihuatanejo. At one point in eastern Oaxaca the mountains subside, and the land between the Gulf of Mexico and the Pacific narrows to only 200 km (126 miles). This place is called the Isthmus of Tehuantepec and was at one time considered as an alternative site for building what would become the Panama Canal (and is now the site of an ambitious project to move goods overland via road and rail between the Pacific Ocean and the Gulf of Mexico). Beyond Oaxaca is Chiapas, the southernmost state in Mexico, a land of mountains and lowland jungles. In the mountains you find the villages of the highland Maya surrounding the town of San Cristóbal. In the jungles you find the ruins of Palenque to the north, and the ruins of Yaxchilán and Bonampak to the southeast, along the border with Guatemala.

Stretching northeast of Chiapas is the large Yucatán peninsula – a low, flat land of tropical forests growing in thin soil above a slab of limestone. The distinguishing feature of the land is that it is honeycombed by underground rivers that on occasion rise to the surface to form perfectly round natural wells called *cenotes*. The peninsula borders the Caribbean on its eastern shore (location of the large resort town of Cancún and the islands of Cozumel and Isla Mujeres) and the Gulf of Mexico on its northern and western shores. In the interior are the ruined Maya cities of Chichén Itzá and Uxmal among others, and the very lively colonial city of Mérida.

Today, despite almost five centuries of racial intermixing and acculturation, there are still five million Indians in Mexico who speak their native language, and close to a million of them who don't speak Spanish. The most numerous Indian-language speakers are Nahuatl (the Aztec language), Maya, Mixtec, Zapotec, Tarahumara, and Purépecha. There are, in addition, many smaller Indian groups in Mexico and about 50 other Indian languages. These various Indian cultures have over the centuries exerted a profound influence on the national culture of Mexico. The Indians, however, simply go about doing what they have been doing for centuries. Many are quite comfortable moving about outside their native regions, finding work where they can, but they draw the distinction between themselves and the people they call Mexicans. Yet for some Indians that distinction is blurred when they establish a household outside their native village or marry someone of a different ethnic group. They or their children then gradually become *mestizos* (the product of intermixing of Spanish and Indian) and join the vast majority of the Mexican population.

In Mexico, this intermixing of the Spanish and Indian races has been a centuries-long process. More than the mixing of races, it has been a mixing of cultures. The particularly strong Indian influence has given a vitality to the national mestizo culture of Mexico that sets it apart from the other Latin American countries where the intermixing has been less thorough, and it allows Mexico to hold its own against cultural encroachments from abroad. Spaniards and South Americans borrow repeatedly from the inventory of slang expressions and word-play of Mexican Spanish, with its sing-song cadences, its large number of native words, and its inventive phras-

A group of Mayans in Zinacantán, Chiapas. There are five million Mexican Indians who still speak their native languages.

ing. Mexican music has also been widely exported, as have Mexican movies and television shows. Mexicans, then, tend to export more culture than they import, and as a result the traveler gets the sense that these are people who enjoy who they are.

One powerful aspect of Mexican culture is its own particular form of Catholicism. Mexicans are active practitioners of their faith. Churches in Mexico don't feel like remnants of a past era; they are much frequented, attracting large crowds. The Mexican form of worship emphasizes prayer, penance, pilgrimages, vigils, and many festivals, and it owes much to the Indian influence, as can be seen in the celebration of the Day of the Dead. This and other religious festivals are the most outward manifestation of this faith, and they are particularly fascinating to witness. Every community has a patron saint who has his/her own feast day, celebrated with much hoopla, and often with rituals that are particular to that town and no other. Add the other favorite saints' feast days, plus the holidays of the civil calendar, and it is clear that Mexicans have many occasions to celebrate.

Religious festivals are just one of several factors that reinforce social cohesion. Another is family. The extended family is highly prized in Mexico, and distant kinship relations are kept alive. Family ties are also extended through forms of ritual kinship such as the famous Mexican institution of *compadrazgo* (co-parenthood), which establishes a relationship between men and women as *compadres* and *comadres,* and cuts across social and class divisions.

As members of a society with a strong sense of local community, of family, and of religion, Mexicans have a clear sense of identity and of place. Of course, there are factors operating in the opposite direction, too. The economy seems to have a disastrous crisis every decade; divorce rates, though still low, are increasing; and Mexico is becoming a more mobile society (more families are moving out of their local communities). It's difficult to tell how all of this will affect Mexican society at large, but with such a strong, exuberant national culture and heritage, how the society responds will be uniquely Mexican.

Facts and Figures

Geography. With an area of 1,987,183 sq km (761,530 sq miles) Mexico is about the half the size of Western Europe, or a fifth the size of the USA. The border with its northern neighbor is 3,326 km (2,065 miles) long, and it has a coastline of almost 9,500 km (6,000 miles) along the Pacific Ocean and the Gulf of Mexico. On the south, it borders on Belize and Guatemala. Mexico is a mountainous country; half its territory is above 900 m (3,000 ft) and volcanic peaks rise well above 5,000 m (16,350 ft) – the highest, the Pico de Orizaba, reaches to 5,700 m (18,640 ft).

Population. Ninety-three million, of whom about 88 million are mestizo (mixed European and Indian blood) and 5 million are Indian. Ninety-five percent are Roman Catholic. Population growth has slowed from 3.5 percent per year in the 1970s to 2 percent at present.

Capital. Mexico City, population 23 million.

Major cities. Guadalajara (5.5 million), Monterrey (3 million), Acapulco (2.8 million), Puebla (2 million), Tijuana (1.5 million).

Government. A Federal Republic, Estados Unidos Mexicanos, created under the Constitution of 1917 and composed of 31 states and the Distrito Federal, which includes the capital. The President is elected for six years, one term only. A Chamber of Deputies is elected for three years and a Senate for six years. The Partido Revolucionario Institucional (PRI), which dominated politics since the 1930s, lost the presidential election to the Partido Acción Nacional (PAN) in 2000.

Economy. Thirty percent of the population is engaged in agriculture, producing exports of coffee, cotton, fruit, and vegetables, but the country has to import the staple food, maize (corn), to meet its needs. Industry, such as manufacturing steel, automobiles, chemicals, textiles, clothing, and assembling electronic parts for US manufacturers, occupies more than half the workforce. Mexico is the world's fourth-largest oil producer, with reserves of some 67 billion barrels. It leads the world in silver mining and is a leader in mining other minerals as well. Tourism attracts more than 19.3 million visitors a year and earns almost US$800 million a year.

A BRIEF HISTORY

The history of Mexico is more a story of revolution than evolution. A sweeping view of history from the earliest civilizations up to the present finds a pattern that keeps repeating itself: A civilization flourishes, weakens, and collapses, or is put to the sword by invaders. As the nation enters a new century, this pattern seems to be changing – and for the better.

Pre-Columbian Cultures

Before any civilization inhabited this land, there were nomadic bands that subsisted by hunting and gathering. The prevailing theory on how they got here credits their ancestors with crossing over a land bridge across what is now the Bering Strait from Siberia to Alaska 15,000 to 20,000 years ago. From Alaska, they moved southwards, arriving in what is now Mexico at least 10,000 years ago.

By around 4,000 B.C. these hunter-gatherers discovered how to domesticate plants, among them maize. In the ensuing centuries, agricultural techniques were refined and extended to other crops, which in turn allowed for the settlement of large communities. By around 1200 B.C. a remarkable civilization emerged in the fertile lowlands along the Gulf Coast in what are now the Mexican states of Veracruz and Tabasco. We call these people the "Olmec," and their civilization was a mother culture for all the peoples that came afterwards.

We have gleaned what we know of the Olmec from their ruined cities, their hieroglyphic writing system, and their distinctive, highly stylized art, which includes the famous stone heads that weigh many tons and portray human features that on some heads look baby-faced and on others feline. They also left beautiful objects carved in jade. The Olmec established the cultural traits that would become universals among the many civilizations to come afterwards. They established a writing system, a simple calendar, a ritual ceremony that we call simply the "ball game," and the construction of large ceremonial centers. And in their demise, the Olmec established the pattern for later civilizations to follow – a cataclysmic decline. Before disappearing, however, they greatly influenced the younger civilizations that sprang up in distant parts of Mexico and Central America: the builders of the metropolis of Teotihuacán in the central highlands of Mexico, a people for whom history has no name; the Zapotecs of the southern highlands of the present state of Oaxaca, who built the beautiful ceremonial complex at Monte Albán; and the Maya, who established several city-states in the lowlands of southeast Mexico, Guatemala, and Honduras, including Palenque, Calakmul, and Tikal.

The Indians of the New World flourished while Europe floundered in the Dark Ages.

The rise of these later civilizations define the Classic period of Pre-Columbian civilization in Mexico (A.D. 300 to 900). The Mayan civilization in particular made spectacular achievements: astronomers refined the calendar to an astonishing level of accuracy, mathematicians invented the "zero," and scribes developed the epigraphic writing system that incorporated phonetics and prefixes and suffixes to indicate elaborate verb tenses. This was a cosmopolitan age that saw great cultural and material exchange between distant city-states. The artis-

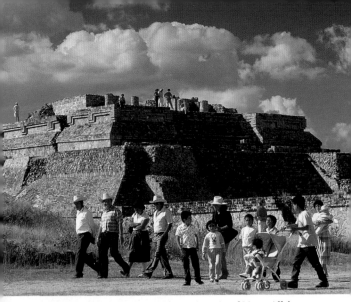

Pre-Columbian souvenirs: The ancient city of Monte Albán recalls a glorious Zapotec past.

tic achievement of the Classic period includes the grandest architecture of the Pre-Columbian era, as a visit to Teotihuacán, Palenque, or Monte Albán quickly confirms. Later cities would be built on as grand a scale, but they wouldn't show the refinement in aesthetic expression – found, too, in sculptures, frescoes, and ceramics – of this earlier age. The city of Teotihuacán held the preeminent position. Evidence suggests that the city had various wards that were occupied by people from several distant lands and of different ethnic groups. At its zenith, Teotihuacán was in all likelihood the largest city in the world. It is here where we see come to prominence the cult of the feathered serpent (later to be known as Quetzalcóatl).

Then, it all came to an abrupt end. Teotihuacán was abandoned. There are signs of violence, but we do not know who inflicted it. The Zapotec culture that built Monte Albán likewise weakened and withdrew in the face of aggression from the neighboring Mixtec. The classic Maya cities were abandoned, too, and other Maya cities to the north in the Yucatán rose in their stead. At the close of the Classic period a people known as the Toltecs began to flourish and filled the vacuum left by the abandonment of Teotihuacán. Their capital was at Tollán (Tula) in the present state of Hidalgo north of the valley of Mexico. They rose to prominence in the 10th century and collapsed by the end of the 12th century. The Toltec put greater emphasis on warfare and human sacrifice than earlier societies had and were more militaristic. But they were great traders as well, following many of the same routes established by the traders of Teotihuacán to distant parts of Mexico. There is obvious Toltec influence in the Post-classic Maya cities of the upper Yucatán, especially Chichén Itzá, which has a number of buildings that are startlingly similar to Tollán and a clear departure from Mayan architecture. But there is a debate as to how this influence was exerted.

In the Toltec pantheon, the plumed serpent, Quetzalcóatl (who represented to some degree knowledge and humanism), and his rival, Tezcatlipoca (lord of the smoking mirror, who represented sorcery and the night), were all-important. Early in the history of Tollán, there seems to have been some civil strife that resulted in the expulsion of a segment of society whose leadership was identified with Quetzalcóatl. In the language of myth, it was said that the god himself was made drunk and shamed by his rival and was forced to leave Tollán. He sailed off to the east, from which he vowed to return someday. This myth was to become one of history's strangest twists – when the Spaniards arrived five centuries later, they were confused with Quetzalcóatl.

A century after the decline of the Toltec, a people known as the Aztec, or the Mexica, came to the central valley of Mexico. For them, warfare held an even more glorified position than it had for the

Toltecs. The valley of Mexico at that time (as it still does) held the greatest concentration of people in Mexico, distributed among several city-states that ringed three large lakes. At first, the Aztec survived as mercenaries for different city-states, eventually adopting much of the culture and refinement of these societies. They established their capital, Tenochtitlán, in the middle of the lake, and, within less than a century, through shrewd alliances and well-planned military campaigns, made themselves masters of entire valley. By the time the Spaniards arrived, Tenochtitlán was an impressive metropolis linked to the shore by great elevated causeways and criss-crossed by canals, in which there was a great traffic of boats.

The Aztec empire kept expanding, waging ever more distant wars across the central highlands and down to the lowlands in the east and into the southern mountain areas of Oaxaca and beyond. Warfare was almost a continuous occupation. In time, war became a ritualized affair made necessary by the need to take prisoners who would satisfy the Aztec gods' need for human sacrifice. At the time of the arrival of the conquistadors, the empire was being racked by crisis: population pressures in the valley were extremely high, relations between Tenochtitlán and its partner cities were tense, the Aztec ruling class was divided, and military expansion had slowed.

The Conquest and the Colonial Era

When the 600 Spaniards arrived at the gulf coast of central Mexico in 1519, they had, from their talks with coastal Indians, a general idea of the scope of the Aztec Empire that awaited them inland. Hernán Cortés, the Spanish leader, was a shrewd campaigner with an instinctual understanding of the hearts of men. In the conquest of this land, he eventually used this talent to manipulate every party who played a role: the soldiers under him; his superior, the Governor of Cuba; the Spanish

The last Aztec ruler, Moctezuma. Formidable as it was, the Aztec Empire nonetheless proved no match for the Spanish colonists.

military force that was later sent against him; the Indian rulers of the cities that paid tribute to the Aztec; Moctezuma, the Aztec ruler; and even the Spanish King Carlos V. With him was Doña Marina, an Indian slave who was presented to Cortés as a gift, and who became his interpreter, his confidant, and his mistress. She is known in Mexico today as La Malinche, a great betrayer of her people, but this is grossly unfair.

One of the first things that Cortés did was burn his ships to prevent his men from considering retreat. Next, he entered into negotiations with Moctezuma, who sent envoys with gifts to persuade Cortés not to come to Tenochtitlán. Moctezuma was an indecisive and superstitious man. Unlike rulers before him, he had been a priest and was more in awe of omens and prophecies than his warriors. He was fully aware of the prediction of Quetzalcóatl's return and wished to keep the white men at a distance until he could decide what to do. His gifts only whetted the Spaniards' appetite for treasure. Cortés made use of Moctezuma's indecision, alternately cajoling and bullying his way to the Aztec capital, while stopping to make allies of the Aztecs' enemies.

The Spaniards arrived in Tenochtitlán in November of 1519, and were greeted with much pomp and ceremony. Cortés soon afterwards made a hostage of the Aztec ruler, hoping to somehow wrest control of the empire from him. Then came a notice of the landing of a second Spanish force with orders to take Cortés prisoner for disobeying his superior. Cortés quickly marched with a portion of his forces to meet the challenger and persuade him to join his endeavor. While gone, a bloody incident occurred that forced the Spaniards to flee the Aztec city with tremendous losses. Moctezuma was killed, either stoned by his own people or killed by the Spanish.

Cortés regrouped the Spanish forces and, with the help of their Indian allies, began slowly to gain military control over the highlands until he isolated Tenochtitlán and could lay siege to it. With the fall of the city, Aztec power ceased and the colonialization of New Spain (as it was called) began. In the Spanish victory died Mexico's 3,000-year-old cultural tradition dating back to the Olmec.

Temples were torn down and the stone was used to build churches and Spanish palaces. Native books were burned and golden ornaments were melted into ingots and sent to Madrid.

The king rewarded Cortés for his actions with wealth, land grants, and a title of nobility, while at the same time shifting control of the colony to a governing council. For the next three centuries, Spain would govern Mexico as a colony. It built the colonial capital on the ruins of Tenochtitlán, set out expeditions in all directions to look for more wealth and to extend the borders of the colony, and issued to its Spanish subjects land grants, known as *encomiendas,* which also provided a compliment of Indian serfs. Soon after the conquest, gold and great quantities of silver ore were found in the mountains north and west of Mexico City, and the Spanish quickly founded several mining towns that were to become beautiful colonial cities.

The church became involved in the colony from the beginning. It faced the enormous task of bringing the teachings of the Christianity to millions of "heathen" natives. Large numbers of evangelizing priests crossed to the New World to be part of this mission. What they found horrified many, including Bishop Bartolomé de las Casas, who fought for the protection and rights of the Indians. Missions established by the church protected the Indians and their lands from encroachment by Spaniards. Many clerics learned the language and customs of their new wards and have written valuable works describing what they found. With Indian labor, the Church erected churches, hospitals, and convents that are some of the most beautiful buildings in the country. For the most part, the Indians embraced the new religion with fervor, and the vast majority remain Roman Catholic to this day.

The Spaniards brought with them cattle, sheep, pigs, chickens, and horses (only the turkey and dog were native to Mexico – even mice came from Europe), sugar cane, bananas, and oranges. Mexico in return gave Europe tomatoes, maize, vanilla, avocados, chocolate, and peanuts. The Spaniards also brought diseases with them, for which the native population had no natural defenses: smallpox, chicken pox, and different varieties of measles, as well as malaria from Africa brought in with slaves. The native population suffered a cataclysmic decline that reached its lowest level in the mid-17th century. In contrast, the population of mixed races, especially the *mestizo* population (the offspring of the union of European and Indian races) grew steadily throughout the colonial era. Above them in the hierarchy of colonial society were the *criollos* (people of European descent born in the New World) and at the top of the ladder were *peninsulares* (Spaniards born in the Old World), who had the trust of the Spanish crown.

Independence

Friction between the criollos and the peninsulares grew steadily as the criollos found themselves excluded from power. Then, in 1810, a criollo village priest, Father Miguel Hidalgo, gave the famous "grito," the cry for independence, in the small town of Dolores, near present-day San Miguel Allende. From Dolores, with his rag-tag peasant army, Hidalgo marched to Guanajuato, where he laid siege to the town's granary-turned-fortress, the Alhóndiga, and won his

Cortés enslaves the Indians – famed Mexican artist, Diego Rivera, captures a slice of Mexico's brutal history in mosaic.

first victory. To this day, the Alhóndiga shows the scars from that battle and impresses the viewer with its formidable walls which must have proved daunting indeed to any besieging force lacking artillery. The movement soon became a full-fledged revolt that was only put down by the government after great difficulty and the execution of Hidalgo and his lieutenants.

But from this effort sprang others, notably the military campaigns waged by the mestizo priest José María Morelos in southern and western Mexico. This was a more convincing and more radical attack on colonial society than Father Hidalgo's struggle, and it horrified the conservative colonial elite, who dedicated enormous resources towards isolating Morelos's forces and cutting off his supply lines. Morelos was finally defeated and executed in 1815, but not before he had introduced the issues of democratic election and the redistribution of land into the political discourse of the day. After his death, the movement for independence, which had until now been the work of the liberals, became a marginal force. But, in an ironic twist, a liberal government came to power in Spain in 1820 and drove the conservative royalists to join the ranks of those fighting for independence.

It was left to the criollo leader of the royalist forces, Agustín de Iturbide, to effect independence in a smooth manner, which he did by uniting his forces with those of the independence movement. The Spanish viceroy was left with no alternative but to abandon his office and return to Spain. After a brief period under the dictatorship of Iturbide, Mexico attempted a republican form of government but with little success. Political struggles between the different parties – centralist/federalist, conservative/liberal – prevented any stable government. In the next 42 years Mexico had 58 presidents. Antonio López de Santa Anna, a man of his times, held the presidency on 11 different occasions. These internal struggles, in addition to poor leadership and the consequences of the long fight for independence, sapped Mexico's energy and made the country vulnerable to foreign incursions. An extortionist expedition by the French blockaded Veracruz in 1838, and Mexico lost half its territory in a disastrous war with the United States in 1848. The loss included the present-day states of Texas, Colorado, Montana, Wyoming, Idaho, Oregon, Washington, California, Nevada, New Mexico, Arizona, and Utah.

Throughout the 1850s the struggle for control of the Mexican government pitted the Conservatives, who favored the large land-holders and the church, against the Liberals, who held to the ideas of 19th-century liberalism and represented the mestizo majority and small businessmen. They advocated an end to the privileges enjoyed by the church and the *hacendados* (owners of haciendas or large landholdings). In the Constitution of 1857, the Liberals managed to get several anticlerical measures passed into law that required the church to sell off its vast landholdings. As a result, rich Mexicans and foreign speculators gained possession of lands that the church had traditionally allowed Indian communities to cultivate.

In the last part of the decade, a civil war broke out and ended in victory for the Liberals. Benito Juárez, one of the most fascinating figures of Mexican history, became president. Juárez, a Zapotec Indian orphaned at three, did not speak Spanish until the age of 12. Educated for the priesthood in Oaxaca, he turned to law and in time became governor of Oaxaca state and drafter of the anticlerical provisions of the 1857 Constitution. Juárez inherited a difficult situation. With the National Treasury empty, he had to suspend payment on the debt claims that foreign powers, including Spain, Britain, and France, held against Mexico. Napoleon III, the emperor of France, sought to extend French influence in the Americas and used this failure to meet payments as a cause for invading Mexico.

His first attempt, however, was not a success. On 5 May 1862 (celebrated as *cinco de mayo*), a poorly equipped and small Mexican army managed to defeat a superior and well-armed French invasion force at Puebla. The French, however, were back by the next year with an even larger force and took control of Mexico City, installing a supporter of France's goals in Mexico, Maximilian of Habsburg, as Emperor. Juárez set up a government in the provinces, doing what

People's hero; a statue in Zacatecas commemorates revolutionary commander Pancho Villa, who helped overthrow dictator Díaz.

he could to wage a guerrilla war against the occupying forces until the French, exhausted by the effort of trying to keep order in Mexico, withdrew their forces and abandoned Maximilian to his fate. He was executed in Querétaro in 1867.

Juárez was reinstalled as president and immediately set to work restoring the economy and improving conditions in the countryside.

By then, Mexico had lived through more than 50 years of constant political strife, been occupied twice by foreign invasion forces, and had suffered several civil wars. In five short years, Juárez managed to establish order and stability and economic development within the country. He died of natural causes in 1872. Four years later, General Porfirio Díaz came to power in a coup d'état. He held on to power for the next 34 years, a period known in Mexico as the Porfiriato. During this time, economic development, especially the construction of railroads and mining and oil drilling, boomed. Foreign investment increased; showy public construction projects such as theaters and opera houses were carried out in cities across the country. But these advances did little to benefit the poor, who were exploited in some parts of the country in the most inhumane manner. Harsh social conditions prevailed in rural areas, where the poor were forced off the land they had worked for themselves and were made into wage laborers for haciendas. The hacendados paid very little and would make sure the workers couldn't leave by providing foodstuffs, clothing, and drink on credit to bind them to the hacienda through debt peonage. These conditions created a large mass of people with little to lose and a lot to avenge.

It was dissatisfaction with Díaz among the middle and the provincial upper classes that eventually put an end to the Porfiriato. Mexicans of the landed classes resented the sweet government deals given to the railroads and other foreign-owned companies. They also resented Díaz's stranglehold on power, which he held as a dictator, with the formality of rigged elections every four years.

The Revolution and Modern Times

In response to the call of Francisco I. Madero, the exiled former governor of Coahuila who had been Díaz's main opposition in the last election, armed revolts broke out in several parts of the country on 20 November 1910. Pancho Villa, in the northern state of Chihuahua, and Emiliano Zapata, in the southern state of Morelos, were the most famous of the revolutionary commanders. So ill-prepared were Díaz's forces for a broad-based insurrection that within six months the dictator was on a boat headed for exile and Madero was installed as the new president of Mexico. For Madero, the cause of the Revolution was to provide such democratic reforms such as one-term offices for presidents, but for a majority of those in the ranks of the revolutionary forces, the causes were workers' rights, an end to debt peonage, land reform, and other social issues. However, before conflict on these issues could crystallize, Madero was betrayed and murdered by his chief of staff, Victoriano Huerta, who assumed control of the government. The revolutionary forces under Zapata and Villa, along with lvaro Obregón and Venustiano Carranza, the governor of Coahuila, returned to the battlefield. In a series of violent, hard-fought victories, Villa and the other commanders destroyed the federal forces and drove Huerta into exile. In these and subsequent conflicts, acts of cruelty were committed on both sides, and human life was held cheap. It is estimated that two million Mexicans died in the Mexican Revolution.

Now it was Carranza's turn to become president. He came from the same educated, landholding class of northern Mexico that Madero did and was just as conservative on social issues, especially land reform. A constitutional assembly was convened to hash out the differences between the different sides. It failed, and conflict arose between Villa, Zapata, and Carranza. Zapata (and only Zapata) remained true to the idea of land reform and didn't see in Carranza a friend of the people. Villa, due to his great popularity, was a threat to Carranza's power. Hostilities broke out, and after some initial victories, Pancho Villa was defeated by Obregón and banished to Chihuahua. Zapata, always staying close to his power base in Morelos, couldn't be beaten, so Carranza found a way to lure him out into the open and murder him. This cost Carranza his political support and made it impossible for him to keep the presidency. He was murdered in rural Veracruz while trying to flee the country.

Obregón succeeded Carranza. He gave social reform plenty of lip service but did little more than make token gestures. During Obregón's presidency, Pancho Villa was assassinated in Chihuahua. Obregón was succeeded by Plutarco Elías Calles, a shrewd man who may have been involved in Obregón's subsequent assassination (when Obregón broke one of the tenets of the Revolution by running for president a second time in an attempt to succeed Calles). This left Calles as the government's strong-man. He established the foundations for the government party that became the Partido Revolucionario Institucional (Instituted Revolutionary Party, or PRI). He also established the system of one-party rule and proceeded to govern Mexico through a succession of puppet presidents until Lázaro Cárdenas forced him into exile in 1936. Once this was done, Cárdenas began fulfilling many of the promises of the Revolution, especially land reform and the nationalization of the foreign-owned oil industry. He became a wildly popular figure and remains so to this day in many parts of the country.

Cárdenas stepped down at the expiration of his term in 1940 and retired from party politics. This set a pattern through which the PRI maintained political stability and the smooth transition of power through an orderly succession of presidents. Each president enjoyed one six-year term in which he dictated the actions of the national government with few constraints. In the fifth year, he personally chose his successor, who would begin a vigorous national political campaign with all the trappings of a democratic electoral contest (though until recently, the outcome of the election was never in doubt). On the sixth year, the president retired from government (in many cases, with a large personal fortune, the source of which is never quite revealed).

By the end of the century, the one-party system was being strained by changes in Mexican society, especially the strengthening of the middle class and the growing independence of a large national business sector. The urban poor and the peasants demonstrated political muscle with shows of strength by a peasant army in Chiapas known as the Zapatistas, and large demonstrations by several organizations of the poor in the capital. In addition, a series of economic crises and political scandals weakened the PRI enough to open political space for two credible opposition parties – the conservative PAN, which has its base in the relatively rich northern half of the country, and the leftist PRD, led by Lázaro Cárdenas's son, Cuauhtémoc. These parties stripped the PRI of its legislative majority and gained control of several state governments. The PRI has responded by democratizing itself. Under its leader President Ernesto Zedillo the party held political primaries in several states to allow the rank and file, not the bosses, to choose the party's candidates.

For the presidential election in the year 2000, Zedillo refused to name a candidate and, instead, established a procedure for holding primary elections across the country. For the first time in more than seven

Monumento a la Revolución in Mexico City commemorates the 1910 movement that led to the modern democracy.

decades, the PRI lost the presidential election to the Partido Acción Nacional (PAN). Many believe that the new president, Vicente Fox, can find solutions to many of the country's social and economic problems. So far, it appears as if Mexico may, for the first time in its history, use political evolution rather than revolution to bring about a new system of government.

Historical Highlights

1000–300 B.C. The flourishing of the Olmecs, the first civilization and the mother culture of pre-Columbian Mexico.

A.D. 300–800 The age of the classic pre-Columbian civilizations of Mexico (Teotihuacán, the Maya, and the Zapotec) and age of great artistic and intellectual evolution.

900–1230 The Toltecs establish their capital at Tollán and control most of central Mexico after the collapse of Teotihuacán. Their influence extends all the way to the Yucatán, especially in the Mayan city of Chichén Itzá.

1350–1519 The Aztec control all of central and southern Mexico from their highland capital of Tenochtitlán.

1521 Hernán Cortés conquers Mexico for the Spanish crown.

1521–1821 Spain rules the colony through a succession of viceroys. The church actively converts the Indians to Christianity. Silver is discovered in great quantities, making Spain the richest country in Europe.

1810 The priest Miguel Hidalgo initiates the struggle for independence from Spain.

1821 Agustín de Iturbide gains independence for Mexico and soon afterwards makes himself emperor.

1823–1861 A period of political turmoil and civil wars.

1848 Mexico is defeated in a war with the US and surrenders over half its territory.

1862–1864 French invasion of Mexico and the establishment of Maximilian as Emperor of Mexico. Defeated by Mexican Nationalist forces under Benito Juárez.

1876–1910 Ruled of dictator Porfirio Díaz, who encourages foreign investments, especially in the construction of railroads.

1910–1929 The Mexican Revolution, which calls for reforms in the name of social equality, and no re-election.

1938 Lázaro Cárdenas expropriates American and British oil companies and nationalizes railroads and all mineral resources.

1988–1999 Political, electoral reforms weaken one-party rule.

2000 First primary presedential elections held across the country.

WHERE TO GO

We use Mexico City as our starting point, then describe side trips and regional itineraries. Wherever your travels in Mexico take you, even a brief visit to Mexico City is in order. Getting to know the thriving capital is the only way to truly understand this captivating country – veiled in mysticism, infused with an appreciation of the present moment, and proud of its colorful heritage.

MEXICO CITY

South of the Río Grande, when people talk about "Mexico," they mean Mexico City, one of the great cities of the world. With a history extending over 2,000 years, Mexico City has served as a center of culture and commerce for ancient civilizations, European conquistadors, and modern Latin America. The country's capital is center stage for all aspects of national life – political, financial, intellectual, and social. It is a magnet that has drawn nearly one out of five Mexicans to its 350 sprawling *colonias,* the elegant suburbs, crowded neighborhoods, and ramshackle squatter settlements that hold an estimated 23 million souls. Big as it is, Mexico City is not a metropolis that overpowers, although recent economic hardships have led to a significant increase in crime. Mexico City is a remarkable place to visit and, with a wealth of historical and cultural attractions, well worth exploring. Most of its attractions for the tourist are easy to visit, since they lie along the 5-km (3-mile) long axis between the Bosque de Chapultepec park and the Zócalo.

The Zócalo

The official name of this central square is the Plaza de la Constitución, but most residents refer to it as *zócalo,* or pedestal, which was all that remained when an equestrian statue of Spain's King Carlos IV was removed after independence. Now, central plazas all over Mexico are informally called "the zócalo."

The vast, unadorned square (240 m/792 ft on each side) covers the very center of what used to be Tenochtitlán, the city the Aztecs founded in 1325. With its solitary flagpole bearing a massive Mexican flag, the constant buzz of activity, and the grandeur of its surrounding buildings – which include the remains of an Aztec pyramid, an ornate colonial cathedral, the stoic center of national government, and towering, modern structures in the background – the zócalo imparts a sense of the layers of history and culture that combine to make modern Mexico.

The zócalo stands on the site of an Aztec market that was once bordered by brightly painted pyramids and palaces. Here is how Bernal Díaz del Castillo, one of Cortés' soldiers, described it: "We were astounded at the great number of people and the quantities of merchandize… dealers in gold, silver, and precious stones, feathers,

View across the zócalo of Mexico City to the Catedral Metropolitana and the Palacio Nacional.

cloaks, and embroidered goods, and male and female slaves… chocolate merchants… those who sold sisal cloth and ropes and the sandals they wear on their feet… Then there were the fruit sellers, and the women who sold cooked food, flour and honey cake and tripe… pottery of all kinds…timber, boards, cradles, beams, paper, and some reeds that smell of liquid amber and are full of tobacco… Some of our soldiers who had been in many parts of the world, in Constantinople, in Rome, and all over Italy, said that they had never seen a market so well laid out, so large, so orderly, and so full of people."

Much as the conquistadores admired the market and the rest of Tenochtitlán, they demolished the city, filling in the canals to make streets and using the Aztec stone to build the metropolis that has grown into present-day Mexico City. They called the open center the Plaza de Armas, a military parade ground.

The **Catedral Metropolitana and Sagrario** (sanctuary), on the north end of the square, was begun in 1573, and by the time the towers were completed in 1813 it incorporated the styles of many architects and artists, inside and out. The north and west sides reflect the austerity of 16th-century Castille; Baroque and Neoclassical elements appear in the main, southern façade; Rococo breaks loose in some of the interior chapels, notably in the Altar de los Reyes. This "Altar of the Kings" is an intricate concoction of carved wood covered with gold leaf, harboring many a hand-wringing saint with eyes cast heavenward, and paintings darkened by age and smoke. The cathedral is big, as befits its site and role, and incorporates 51 domes, including the central cupola designed by Manuel Tolsá. Many of the 14 chapels were damaged in a 1967 fire, but have been restored. The second on the right holds the black Cristo del Veneno (Christ of the Poison). Details vary, but basic legend has it that a local bishop who had been poisoned was saved when he kissed the image, which drew out the venom, shriveled up, and turned black. The last chapel on the left is dedicated to San Felipe de Jesús, the first Mexican saint, who was martyred in 1597 attempting to convert

The Lay of the Land

Getting around Mexico City is no problem. Unless you hit the rush hours, the ride in from Benito Juárez airport takes no more than half an hour on the expressway, the Periférico, that surrounds the city. Main exits are to avenues marked as *ejes*, or axes, which run from the periphery to central zones. The city streets, as in most Mexican cities and towns, form a grid – a pattern introduced by Spain in colonial times. Mexicans thwart this orderly layout by changing some street names every few blocks to honor a long list of national heroes. Mexico City's neighborhoods have clusters of "theme" street names. The Zona Rosa, the district of boutiques, hotels, and restaurants midway up the Reforma, has streets named after European cities; on the other side of the avenue are river names. In the old town, around the Zócalo, are the country names, while mountains are the feature of the Lomas de Chapultepec suburb. Other colonias commemorate poets, statesmen, scientists, and so on. Thus a street's name often will indicate its location.

The metro covers the city with nine lines and 125 stations. Some attractive stations also function as centers for shopping and socializing. Due to increases in purse snatchings and muggings, its best to avoid the metro during rush hour, or late at night. Among the highly-publicized robbery and murder victims have been tourists who used the metro and buses, as well as the wandering VW bug taxis known as *taxis ecológicos* – most taxi-related crimes have occurred on board these green cabs. The US State Department has posted an official traveler's advisory warning its citizens against hailing cabs off the street, advising them to only travel in *sitio* taxis, preferably assigned to their hotel. Where this adds to the cost of getting around, it's a minimal incremental expense, and well worth it in terms of personal safety and peace of mind. The hotel information desk should be able to give you the correct phone numbers to call. Always make sure that the taxi you board displays a large 5-by-7 inch laminated registration card with a picture of the driver on it.

the Japanese. It also contains the ashes of Augustín de Iturbide, a royalist commander during the movement for independence who declared Mexico an independent country and himself its emperor, and the throne upon which he was crowned.

Tilting away from the Cathedral on the right is El Sagrario, dedicated in 1768 to Santiago (St. James), the patron saint of Mexico City. The two façades and finely carved doors of this smaller church are considered masterpieces of Churrigueresque, the extravagant Baroque style that Spanish architect José Churriguera adopted and adapted throughout 18th-century Mexico. Its Renaissance elements, such as inverted obelisks, Greek columns and pilasters, and garlands and cornices are tumultuously assembled and leave no space empty. The two churches, like a number of other buildings in the central district, have been sinking and sagging for years and are now supported on pilings. Draining the surrounding lake and pumping water have caused the slow collapse of the land on which they "floated." A major restoration effort that included reinforcement of the subsoil has saved the buildings from probable collapse.

Beside the Sagrario, a model of Tenochtitlán sits in a basin of water that represents Lake Texcoco. The three causeways linking the island city with the land intersected at what was the ceremonial center of Moctezuma's empire. The sacred enclosure was 45 m (500 ft) square and held 78 buildings, including the Royal Palace. Just beyond the Sagrario a wall encloses the excavations of the **Templo Mayor**, the pyramid to the Aztec gods of rain and war, Tláloc and Huitzilopochtli. Streets and colonial structures covered the site until 1978, when work on a new metro uncovered a beautifully carved stone disk 3 m (10 ft) in diameter that depicts the moon goddess, Coyolxauhqui, with her head and limbs severed. According to legend, her brother Huitzilopochtli, the sun god, threw her from the top of a hill as punishment for rebellion. The find pinpointed the site of his great temple, for the disk of the dismembered goddess was placed at its base to re-enact her fall and to represent the struggle between the sun and the moon.

Atrium of the Palacio Nacional; the venerable palacio is the seat of government today, as it was in Aztec times.

The ancient Mexicans always enlarged these monuments by building on top of the previous structure, removing nothing. Archaeologists uncovered seven layers of the Templo Mayor and a treasure trove of offerings to the gods underneath. These are displayed in the handsome **Museo del Templo Mayor**. The museum overlooks the site and is divided into sections representing the two temples, which are set on a pyramidal base. The entrance fee includes access to the excavations. The museum's bookshop has one of the best selections of foreign-language titles on Mexican art and antiquity.

Breathing Easy

Despite major steps being taken to alleviate Mexico City's infamous smog (restricted driving, factory closings, emission-controlled buses and taxis), pollution persists, albeit at levels less severe than they were in the past. Mexico City sits in a bowl, surrounded by mountains. More than half of the country's industry and more than a fifth of its population is located in the surrounding area. In winter, a temperature inversion causes emissions, along with dust, to be trapped in the bowl's atmosphere.

For the visitor, dealing with the pollution is a matter of luck and perseverance. On some days you won't notice it; on other days it will make your nose run, eyes water, and throat rasp. The best time to be outdoors or actively walking around is in the evenings, when the air is cooler and relatively clean, or on Sundays, when most factories are closed and traffic is relatively light. If you have respiratory problems, be very careful; the city's elevation makes matters even worse.

To control pollution in the capital, the government has established the Hoy No Circula program, under which cars manufactured prior to 1993 are not allowed to circulate one day of the week, depending on the last number on the license plate. Limitations are more severe on days when pollution is especially heavy. Newspapers and radio and TV news broadcast reports on the levels of carbon monoxide, sulphur, nitrogen oxide, and other gases in the air and compare these with maximum levels for human health, along with the numbers of the license plates that aren't allowed to circulate that day. This is important information, because the program also applies to rental cars and to cars with foreign license plates (if your license plate doesn't have any numbers, then Friday is the day you can't drive your car.) There's a stiff fine for violating this regulation.

The **Palacio Nacional** takes up the east side of the zócalo. This is the seat of government, as indeed it was when the palace of Moctezuma occupied the site. The Aztec emperor kept a collection of animals, water birds, and fish here in what was the first zoo in the Americas. Cortés claimed the entire property and his son, Martín, sold it to Spain. The present structure, begun in 1693 (the Spanish Viceroys lived in an earlier building), has undergone many changes, serving as a prison, army barracks, and home of the first Mexican Congress. Maximilian, the emperor sent by France to govern Mexico during the 1860s, enlarged it, and a third story was added in 1927. The President's office is in an inner courtyard, though he frequently works in his residence, "Los Pinos," in Bosque de Chapultepec.

At 11pm on 15 September, the zócalo fills with people when the President reads Father Hidalgo's declaration of independence, the "Grito de Dolores," from the central balcony. Hanging above him is the liberty bell from Hidalgo's church, which rings in Mexico's national holiday, answered by the great 12-ton bell of the cathedral. The central portal of the Palacio Nacional leads to a patio where a broad staircase ascends beneath Diego Rivera's murals of the history of Mexico. It's all here, with the whole cast of thousands spread out along three walls. The account begins on the right, before the Conquest, with the blonde god Quetzalcóatl sailing across the sky and an upside-down sun god bringing food and life to an Indian world. In the center, violent battles engage the Spaniards with Aztec eagle and jaguar knights. The Church burns Mayan books, but Bishop de las Casas protects the Indians, fending off a conquistador with his crucifix. The Inquisition strangles heretics in dunce caps. White-haired Father Hidalgo rallies the populace for independence. Benito Juárez holds the 1857 Constitution. American soldiers invade Veracruz and Emiliano Zapata proclaims "Tierra y Libertad." On the left, Karl Marx points to the future, while capitalists scheme and Diego Rivera's wife and artist, Frida Kahlo (she of the black eyebrows), represents education as the hope of the people. Other

43

Rivera panels depicting different indigenous tribes encircle the second floor arcade. In one, Malinche, her face hidden, walks behind Cortés, carrying their blue-eyed baby, symbolically the first *mestizo.*

Between the Palacio Nacional and the Suprema Corte (Supreme Court) building to the south is the Acequia Real, once a canal, then a street, and now a likeness of the canal, with grass replacing water. The zócalo's south side is occupied by the Departamento del Distrito Federal (Federal District building) and the old City Hall. On the east, the garden, restaurant, and bar on the roof of the Hotel Majestic offer a terrific view of the whole plaza. Two blocks north is the **Nacional Monte de Piedad** (National Pawn Shop). All around are rooms filled with an amazing collection of unclaimed items on sale. You just might find an attractive antique ring here amid the busts of Beethoven, old radios, and musty sofas.

The Centro Histórico

The zócalo is the heart of the *centro histórico*, old Mexico City. Its streets are studded with colonial palaces and churches, enchanting squares, and many museums. The area behind the cathedral is an ongoing marketplace, with each street known for its particular specialty – be it books, wedding dresses, or sewing machines. For example, hundreds of concoctions from medicinal plants are sold in an alley off Calle República de Guatemala. República de Brasil leads into the Plaza de Santo Domingo, one of the capital's most picturesque corners. Under the arcades, public scribes type documents, fill out complicated government forms, or even compose love letters for illiterate or tongue-tied clients. Here also are the printers who will make up a wedding invitation or business card on their hand presses.

Stop by the 18th-century **Templo de Santo Domingo** to see the chapel on the right with a wall covered with *milagros*, small silver arms, legs, eyes, and other bits of anatomy offered in thanks for recovery from illness. You'll see these *milagros,* also known as *ex-votos*, and *retablos* (primitive paintings on tin) in churches all over the country.

Take Calle Obregón from the square and turn left on Calle Argentina to the **Secretaría de Educación Pública** (Ministry of Public Education). More than a hundred of Diego Rivera's earliest (1923) and best murals cover the walls of the courtyard, staircases, and upper floors of the ministry. Look for the lively *Day of the Dead* scene in the left rear of the patio. While Rivera was at work here, his contemporaries, David Alfaro Siqueiros and José Clemente Orozco, were painting frescos in the **Colegio de San Idelfonso** around the corner (to compare the work of these three Mexican masters, follow Calle Argentina a block toward the zócalo and turn left to 16 Calle Justo Sierra). Orozco's powerful and bitter scenes of injustice and war cover walls on three floors of the inner patio. On Calle de la Moneda, on the north flank of the Palacio Nacional, the first printing press in the western hemisphere was operating in 1536. After the street becomes Calle Zapata, it leads to Empress Carlota's favorite church, **La Santísima**, with a Churrigueresque façade rivalling the Sagrario's.

Three blocks south of the Palacio Nacional on Avenida Pino Suárez, the **Museo de la Ciudad de México** (Mexico City Museum) is housed in the imposing colonial mansion of the Counts of Santiago Calimaya. Water spouts in the form of cannons overhang the street. The museum is a good place to get your bearings – it has excellent topographical maps of the region, the lake, and its Aztec dikes, models and engravings of the city at different stages of growth, and relics from every period. Across the avenue an inscription marks the spot where Moctezuma first met Cortés. Behind it is the **Hospital de Jesús**, founded by Cortés and still functioning. The bust of the founder in the courtyard is one of very few memorials to Cortés in Mexico, where he is regarded as a perpetrator of genocide.

The centro histórico is experiencing a renaissance in nightlife. Despite the fact that the area essentially clears out after dark, a number of hip clubs have opened in exquisite Baroque and Art Deco buildings. Dancing to techno in such a historic ambiance is one of the ambiguous pleasures of Mexico City.

Plaza Garibaldi, at the northern edge of the historic district on the Paseo de la Reforma, remains an important landmark as the gathering place for mariachis. However, the square has earned a new notoriety – it is now known as one of the highest crime areas in Mexico City, a meeting point for young criminals who make their living by separating visitors from their personal belongings. Even so, Plaza Garibaldi is a must-see, perhaps as the first stop on your evening rounds (while the ambiance might not be as lively as it is in the wee hours, the plaza is definitely a lot safer at this time). Mariachis start drifting into the little plaza and will be there until the early hours of the morning. Notice the statues of well-loved popular musicians around the plaza.

For more traditional pleasures, retire to the leafy island of the **Alameda Central**, about six blocks due south of Plaza Garibaldi along the Reforma and next to the Palacio de Bellas Artes. Mexico City's first park was created in the late 16th century by draining a pond and planting the poplar trees (*álamos*), after which it is named. In the 18th and 19th centuries this was the center of fashion, off-limits to the common people. Today it is a favorite place for a Sunday family outing amid romantic statuary and fountains. Huge clusters of fancifully designed balloons bob along in the clutch of vendors, while children clamor for ice cream and lovers embrace on the benches. This is where heretics were burned at the stake during the Inquisition. There are musical performances in the Moorish bandstand on weekends.

The scene is amusingly captured in Rivera's mural *A Dream of a Sunday Afternoon in the Alameda Park*, created for the old Del Prado Hotel on Avenida Juárez, which skirts the southern flank of the plaza. The hotel was wrecked by the 1985 earthquake, but the mural was spared and now has its home in the **Museo Mural Diego Rivera** at the western end of the park. The exhibit documents the fracas that erupted when the mural was unveiled and found to have

A Diego Rivera mural in the Palacio National depicts daily life in Tenochtitlán.

the words *Dios no existe* ("There is no God") on a paper held by one of Rivera's subjects. After much controversy, the offending sentence was removed. Rivera himself appears as a pudgy boy holding the hand of a lady skeleton wrapped in a feathered serpent boa. Next door is the Pinacoteca Virreinal, exhibiting colonial period paintings in a former monastery.

At 89 Avenida Juárez, the **FONART** displays handicrafts from all over Mexico and operates a fixed-price shop. The large marble monument across the way is the Hemiciclo, dedicated to Benito Juárez. Tour guides joke that the **Torre Latino-Americano**, the city's first skyscraper, towering over Avenida Juárez just east of the Alameda, is "the highest skyscraper in the world" – the first of its 42 floors is 2,415 m (7,925 ft) above sea level. The observation deck is a good place to watch the sun go down. Most of the building has been vacated, and there are plans to turn it into a hotel. A monastery founded in 1525 as headquarters of the Franciscan Order once stood here, but it was destroyed in the 19th-century Reform and the sunken **Iglesia de San Francisco** behind the tower is all that's left. A Methodist chapel occupies the cloister.

Museo de Artes e Industrias Populares – detail of "Une Carte des Costumes."

Across the Avenida Hidalgo, the broad avenue that forms the Alameda's northern border, is the **Iglesia de San Hipólito**, known for the statue of San Judas Tadeo, patron saint of lost causes. Also look for the tablet carved in 1599 of an eagle carrying an Indian in its claws. If you follow Avenida Hidalgo west across the Reforma, you'll come to the Hotel Cortés, which occupies a 17th-century building that once provided lodgings to visiting monks. Its attractive patio is a good spot to rest and enjoy a coffee or *cerveza*. Hidalgo, incidentally, follows the path of the causeway that was the exit road on which the Spaniards fought their way out of Tenochtitlán on the Noche Triste, a

Museums

Most museums in Mexico City close on Monday. If the museum listed closes on a day other than Monday, days are indicated. There is usually no entrance fee on Sundays, and museums are accordingly more crowded then than they are at other times. Ask about guided tours at the museum entrances – many offer tours for a small fee, though some are in Spanish only. Note that times listed below can change without notice, especially hours of operation. Also, telephones are usually answered by Spanish speaking personnel, who might not be able to help you in English. The best source of tourist information in English is the Mexico City tourism office at Amheres 54 in the Zona Rosa. They run an information hotline daily 9am–7pm; Tel. (55) 5208-1030.

Museo Anahuacalli. *Calle Museo 150*; Tel. (55) 5677-2873. 10am–2pm and 3–6pm; free. From the Taxqueña metro station take the Tren Ligero to the Xotepingo station. Take the western exit and from Museo walk 9 blocks towards División del Norte.

Museo de Arte Moderno Bosque de Chapultepec. *Tel. (55) 5211-8729*. Open 10am–5.30pm; 15 pesos. Metro Chapultepec or Auditorio.

Museo de la Ciudad de México. *Pino Suárez 30, Centro Histórico*; Tel. (55) 5542-0671. Open 10am–6pm; free. Metro Pino Suárez or Zócalo.

Museo de la Numismática. *Banco de México on Eje Central and 5 de Mayo, First Floor, Centro Histórico*. Open Monday– Friday 10am–6pm; 10 pesos. Metro Bellas Artes.

Museo del Templo Mayor. *Seminario, east of the Catedrál, Centro Histórico*; Tel. (55) 5542-4943. Open 9am–5pm; 35 pesos. Metro Zócalo.

Museo Dolores Olmedo. *Avenida México 5843, La Noria, Xochimilco*; Tel. (55) 5555-1016. Open 10am–6pm; 30 pesos. Metro Taxqueña.

Museo El Caracol. *Bosque de Chalpultepec; Tel. (55) 553-6285.* Open 10am–4.30pm; 30 pesos. Metro Chapultepec.

Museo Estudio Diego Rivera. *Altavista and Diego Rivera, San Ángel; Tel. (55) 5616-0996.* Open 10am–6pm; 10 pesos. Take a bus or microbus that says San Ángel. Get off on Altavista. Walk up Altavista for 6 blocks. Easiest by taxi.

Museo Franz Mayer. *Avenida Hidalgo 45, Centro Histórico; Tel. (55) 5518-2265.* Open 10am–5pm; 20 pesos. Metro Bellas Artes.

Museo Frida Kahlo. *Calle Londres 247, Coyoacán; Tel. (55) 5554-5999.* Open 10am–6pm; 30 pesos. No cameras are allowed. Metro Coyoacán.

Museo León Trotsky. *Viena 45, Coyoacán; Tel (55) 5658-8732.* Open 10am–5pm; 20 pesos. Metro Coyoacán.

Museo Mural Diego Rivera.*Balderas y Colón s/n, Centro Histórico; Tel. (55) 5510-2329.* Open 10am–6pm; 10 pesos. Metro Hidalgo.

Museo Nacional de Antropología. *Bosque de Chapultepec; Tel. (55) 553-6381.* Open 9am–7pm; 35 pesos; 45 pesos fee for video cameras. Metro Auditorio.

Museo Nacional de Arte. *Tacuba 8, Centro Histórico; Tel. (55) 5130-3400.* Open 10.30am–5.30pm; free. Metro Allende.

Museo Nacional de Historia. *Castillo de Chapultepec, Bosque de Chapultepec; Tel. (55) 5553-6224.* Open 9am–4.30pm; 35 pesos. Metro Chapultepec.

Museo Rufino Tamayo. *Bosque de Chapultepec; Tel. (55) 5286-6529.* Open 10am–6pm; 15 pesos. Metro Chapultepec.

Papalote Museo del Niño. *Bosque de Chapultepec, Segunda Sección; Tel. (55) 5237-1773.* Open Monday–Friday 9am–1pm, 2–6pm, Saturday and Sunday 10am–2pm, 3–7pm; 75 pesos. Metro Constituyentes.

night in which the Aztecs dealt a strong blow to the Spanish army, who fled for this one night before returning to conquer the captial.

On the northen side of the Alameda, between two facing churches sunk below the level of Hidalgo, the **Museo Franz Mayer** is beautifully installed in the former San Juan de Dios hospital. Mayer, a German-born businessman, was a collector of all things Mexican: furniture, sculpture, church images, ceramics, and curiosities such as an exquisite mosaic composed of bits of bright feathers. There is a cafeteria and a peaceful patio where you can relax listening to classical music. The church to the right, Santa Vera Cruz, is so steeply tipped that the aisle goes uphill.

The **Palacio de Bellas Artes** (Fine Arts Palace), at the eastern end of the Alameda, is a not-so-fine white marble Victorian pile typical of the grandiose projects of the dictator Porfirio Díaz. The interior, however, has a pure Art Deco rotunda and staircase of the 1920s leading to galleries where you can see murals all in one place by the Big Four of Mexican painting, Rivera, Siqueiros, Orozco, and Tamayo. The ever-popular Ballet Folklórico de México stages a program of regional dances here in a theater famed for a Tiffany curtain made

Marble sculpture lines the façade of the Palacio de Bellas Artes.

from thousands of pieces of stained glass depicting Popocatépetl and Iztaccíhuatl. Light played on the curtain recreates dawn and sunset on the mountains. Because of the weight of the curtain, it is not lowered for every performance.

The central post office is just across the Avenida Lázaro Cárdenas from the Bellas Artes and just beyond it, on Calle Tacuba, is **the Museo Nacional de Arte**. The collection is heavy on 19th-century works, but there are interesting pieces from pre-Conquest times. The statue in front is El Caballito (the Little Horse), whose pedestal gave the zócalo its name. Coin collectors will enjoy the **Museo de la Numismática** on the first floor of the Banco de México building adjoining the post office.

Three blocks south of the Museum, on Calle Madero, is the **Casa de los Azulejos**, built in 1596 for the Count of Valle de Orizaba and covered in 18th-century blue tiles from Puebla. The Sanborns restaurant chain has converted the elegant inner court into a restaurant where homesick gringos flock to get a solid breakfast and hamburgers. You'll be served under a balcony where the suitor of the daughter of Valle de Orizaba was hanged after murdering the Count on the staircase. Down the street at number 17 is the **Palacio de Iturbide**, where the general was proclaimed Emperor of Mexico in 1822. The palace now houses a bank, but frequent temporary exhibits are held on the beautiful patio.

Two of the city's liveliest handicraft markets are a ten-minute walk south of the Alameda. The **Mercado de Artesanías de San Juan** is on Calle Ayuntamiento, just off Calle López, Mexico City's Chinatown. Scores of little shops on two floors of this arcade sell the full range of Mexican crafts. The **Mercado de Artesanías de la Ciudadela** is five blocks down Calle Balderas on the Plaza de la Ciudadela. Here you can watch artisans weaving, painting, and hammering away on their products. La Ciudadela on this square is a former arsenal, now the national library.

About ten blocks east of La Ciudadela on Fray Servando T. de Mier, is one of Mexico's most bewitching markets, the **Mercado de Sonora**. It is an unusual market offering an opportunity to visit the world of magic and spells that surrounds the daily lives of residents of Mexico City. Next to the stalls that sell plastic and ceramic pots, and all the fixings for a successful wedding or birthday party, you can find all manner of magical potions, as well as alum to counteract negative forces, black salt, and candles of every color, for whatever ritual you might be interested in holding. There are experts in love potions and the ever-important *limpias* (cleansings) to dismiss any spell that may have been cast upon you by a jealous lover or an envious co-worker. Tarot card readings and even santería registers are offered here, conducted by real-life shamans. You will also find live black roosters, white hens, and multicolored birds, along with eggs of every color and size. Hundreds of herbs that will cure every ailment are sold in the market, next to amulets and talismans to bring good luck to an enterprize, or guard your house from evil spirits.

North and South along La Reforma

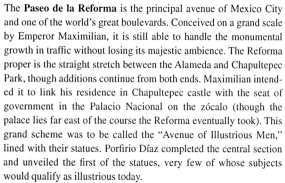

The **Paseo de la Reforma** is the principal avenue of Mexico City and one of the world's great boulevards. Conceived on a grand scale by Emperor Maximilian, it is still able to handle the monumental growth in traffic without losing its majestic ambience. The Reforma proper is the straight stretch between the Alameda and Chapultepec Park, though additions continue from both ends. Maximilian intended it to link his residence in Chapultepec castle with the seat of government in the Palacio Nacional on the zócalo (though the palace lies far east of the course the Reforma eventually took). This grand scheme was to be called the "Avenue of Illustrious Men," lined with their statues. Porfirio Díaz completed the central section and unveiled the first of the statues, very few of whose subjects would qualify as illustrious today.

Agile windshield-washing boys pounce on cars when they stop for the traffic lights on the Reforma. One intersection becomes a stage for jugglers and acrobats, another is the nighttime turf of a kid who takes a mouthful of petroleum from a can and blows out a plume of fire, then runs to collect pesos from drivers. Here and there you may spot one of the few remaining Victorian mansions that once lined the avenue. Now they are in the shadow of some of the hemisphere's most arresting modern office buildings. Look for the new Bolsa, the Stock Exchange, an angular sandwich of two-tone glass layers beside a multifaceted beehive of mirrored panels.

Along the stretch of La Reforma north of the Alameda there are several places of interest, although this area of Mexico City is generally not known for tourist attractions. One popular site is Mexico's main flea market, the **Mercado de la Lagunilla**, found just east of the intersection of the Reforma, with Calle Lázaro Cárdenas at the roundabout marked by the statue of José Martí. Everything imaginable is sold here. This is the place to practice your bargaining and to spend an entertaining Sunday morning.

Monument to victory: Independencia, also known as El Ángel, on the Paseo de la Reforma .

Although the street market takes place only on Sundays, there are a few permanent stalls open the rest of the week as well.

The significance of the **Plaza de las Tres Culturas** is summed up in its name – The Plaza of Three Cultures – and is yet another visual monument to the depth and wealth of Mexican culture and history. It

Honoring the Virgen de Guadalupe

The Virgin of Guadalupe is the true patron saint of Mexico and most of Latin America. Copies of her image are omnipresent throughout Mexico, and even the most sophisticated Mexican is likely to keep a small replica of the Virgin at home. The twelfth of December is the day of the Virgin. Hundreds of thousands of faithful worshipers from all over the world flood the Basílica in Mexico City to pay homage to the Virgin, with many starting their pilgrimages months in advance to arrive in Mexico City on this sacred day. Dancers wearing costumes of Aztec influence, and others wearing the traditional mestizo dress of manta pants and shirts, dance for hours on end until they reach the main square of the temple. It is also common to see people who end their pilgrimage by walking on their knees the whole length of the Calzada de Guadalupe (close to 3 km/2 miles) as a sign of their true devotion to the Virgin, or to thank her for some miracle granted. While there is a festive and mystical air that surrounds the whole event, the occasion is a solemn one, and is one of Mexico's most impressive celebrations. Many other places in Mexico celebrate the day of the Virgin of Guadalupe as well, with processions, fireworks, and other religious and popular displays. Particularly beautiful is the celebration in Puerto Vallarta, which extends from 1–12 December, with nightly processions by different groups in the community. The Virgin of Guadalupe is the patron saint of this town, and the namesake of its famed church.

is near the northeastern end of the Reforma in what was the important Aztec market town of Tlatelolco. The ruins of a temple pyramid are overlooked by the colonial church of San Francisco and the modern glass and steel ministry of foreign affairs, hence, the three cultures. The final battle of the conquest was fought here and a plaque movingly records the event: "On 13 August 1521, heroically defended by Cuauhtémoc, Tlatelolco fell into the hands of Hernán Cortés. It was neither a triumph nor a defeat: it was the painful birth of the mestizo nation that is Mexico today." The apartment houses nearby were badly damaged by the earthquake that rocked Mexico City in 1985.

Continuing out the northern extension of the Reforma known as Calzada de Guadalupe, 4 km (2½ miles) beyond the Plaza de las Tres Culturas you will come to one of the world's great religious shrines and the center of Catholic Mexico, the **Basílica de la Virgen de Guadalupe**. Ten years after the Conquest, a newly baptized Indian named Juan Diego had a vision of the Virgin, who requested that a church be built in her honor on this site (an Aztec temple to the mother of the gods had once stood here but was razed by the Spaniards). The bishop was suspicious of Juan Diego's tale.

Floating festivity: 12 December marks the Catholic festival of La Guadalupe.

The Virgin again appeared to the Indian, instructing him to pick roses and take them to the bishop as proof of the request. Roses miraculously appeared on the rocky hillside and Juan Diego collected them in his cloak. But when he took them to the doubting prelate, instead of roses, the cloak had Mary's image imprinted upon it. Convinced by this miracle, the bishop ordered the church built to display the cloak. The image remains to this day, a mystery to scientists seeking to explain this modest cloth that is more than 450 years old. The present Basílica is the fifth to hold this relic – visitors can view the cloak close up from an underpass beside the altar without disturbing the mass.

The stretch of the Paseo de la Reforma that runs south from the Alameda is lined with many of Mexico City's best-known landmarks. Along this stretch, roundabouts – called *glorietas* – interrupt the avenue. The first, heading southwest from the Alameda, is Colón, the monument to Christopher Columbus; next comes Cuauhtémoc, the last Aztec ruler shaking his spear defiantly; then Independencia, better known as El Ángel for the winged victory atop its column; then the multi-colored glass pillars of a fountain illuminated at night; at the entrance to Chapultepec park, Diana, Goddess of the Hunt, armed with her bow, graces a fountain.

One block to the right of Colón, on Calle Ramírez, the **Monumento a la Revolución** looms over the Plaza de la República, commemorating the movement in 1910 that paved the way for the modern state. The arched cube and dome, part of a legislature building never completed, was salvaged to become the shrine where Pancho Villa and other heroes are buried. Locomotive 67, planted on a platform, commemorates the role of railroad men in the fighting.

To the right of Cuauhtémoc, where Insurgentes crosses the Reforma, Calle Sullivan leads to the **Jardín del Arte**. On Sundays the garden blooms with paintings that artists display for sale; at night, it has become Mexico City's most renowned red-light district. To the left of the avenue is the worldly enclave of the **Zona Rosa**. Here, the streets are named after cities – though you might not recognize Amberes as Antwerp or Niza as Nice. If you need help, this district employs police-men whose badges identify the languages they speak. Pedestrian zones with sidewalk cafés go on for several blocks, lined with attractive bou-tiques, jewelry shops, chic restaurants, and rousing nightclubs. There's a wonderfully cluttered labyrinth of handicraft and food stalls in the Mercado Insurgentes between Londres and Liverpool just off Floren-cia. The concentration of tourist trade has tarnished the Zona Rosa's pretensions to elegance. The fancy shops have moved with the money to the Polanco District, on the right flank of the Bosque de Chapulte-pec, where the newest high-rise luxury hotels are clustered.

Bosque de Chapultepec

Wooded Bosque de Chapultepec (Chapultepec Park) spreads over 400 hectares (988 acres), and as one of the last natural areas in this congested valley is known as the "lungs of the city." It was a royal retreat for the Aztec kings, who are believed to have planted some of the venerable *ahuehuete* trees (a kind of tall cypress) surrounding the hill at the park entrance. They also built an aqueduct to serve Tenochtitlán that ran down what is now Avenida Chapultepec. Cha-pultepec means "Grasshopper Hill" in Náhuatl. The hill has often played a central role in the city's history. Cortés fortified it and the Spanish viceroys built their residence, the **Castillo de Chapultepec**, on its summit (it was a military academy when the US troops of General Winfield Scott stormed the heights in 1847). The monument of six white columns at the base of the hill commemorates Los Niños Héroes, the "boy heroes," cadets who fell in the battle.

The Castillo became the palace of Maximilian and Carlotta and then the residence of a number of Mexican presidents. It has been the Museo Nacional de Historia since 1944. On the ground floor, portraits of leaders and summaries of their political fortunes may end up confusing even the most earnest history student. All the play-ers in the pageant of Mexican history are assembled in a mural by

Juan O'Gorman. Upstairs, David Alfaro Siqueiros does a masterful job of cramming a historical epic on nine walls of two rooms. In one, Porfirio Díaz sits with his foot on the laws; in another Emiliano Zapata reins in his galloping horse just short of the door.

Another ingenious, more easily comprehensible telling of the Mexico story awaits you in the **Caracol**, a snail-shaped glass museum tucked into the hillside, down from the castle entrance. Entering at the top, you descend a spiral corridor lined with small historical dioramas from vice-regal days onward. There is a collection of remarkable photos of the 1910 Revolution. The last turning brings you to a dramatic rotunda of carved stone where the Mexican flag and a sculpture of the eagle and serpent emblem are lit by a shaft of sunlight. After all this walking around, you may be ready to sink into a comfortable chair at the nearby Audiorama, a peaceful garden enclosure where you can relax and on occasion be treated to a free recorded classical music program.

Bosque de Chapultepec was once the preserve of the rich and privileged; now it belongs to the people. On Sundays you'll think all of Mexico City's millions have turned out to picnic on the grass, play ball with the children, row boats on the lakes, and climb on a wooden horse to pose in a Pancho Villa sombrero for a park photographer. The shady walks are lined with food and drink stalls, balloon sellers, and artists painting clown make-up on children's faces. The Zoo here is famous for its four giant pandas, three of whom were bred and born in the zoo, a most unusual occurrence. The noisiest inmates, howler monkeys from the Yucatán jungles, outroar the lions. The President's residence is at the southern end, where an expressway divides the park. On the far side, an amusement park boasts dozens of rides, including a monster rollercoaster called the *montaña rusa*, or Russian mountain. Nearby, you can see how the indefatigable Diego Rivera embellished the city waterworks with a mosaic sculpture-fountain of the rain god, Tláloc, spread-eagled in a basin and spurting water from every pore. Just outside the perimeter of the park is a wonderfully imaginative, hands-on children's museum, **Papalote Museo del Niño**.

Museo Nacional de Antropología

The Museo Nacional de Antropología (Museum of Anthropology) is not only by far the world's greatest collection of early Meso-American art, it is also a brilliant, unforgettable architectural masterpiece. A visit to this treasure house in the Bosque de Chapultepec would alone make the trip to Mexico City memorable. The architect, Pedro Ramírez Vazquez, also designed the Museo del Templo Mayor, the Museo del Caracol, Estadio Azteca, the new Basílica de Guadalupe, and many other Mexico City landmarks. Here he has used local stone and ancient motifs to create a most original modern setting that subtly evokes the past.

Aztec culture is well-represented in the renowned collections of the Museo Nacional de Antropología.

Guarding the entrance is a fourth-century B.C. statue of Tláloc, God of Rain. (When it was moved from its original location across the valley in the 1960s, thunder, lightning, and a downpour broke over the city.) The museum is built around four sides of a court 82 m (268 ft) long that is open to the sky, reminiscent of the ceremonial spaces in pre-Conquest ruins. Overhanging the entrance to the court is an immense aluminum roof that seems to float without support, with sky visible on all sides. This canopy is pierced by a massive column that disappears through a hole. Perpetual "rain" showers from this opening, forming a curtain around the column and the figures that cover it. Unseen above, a steel mast projecting from the column holds the roof up by cables. The court radiates power, mystery, and serenity.

A 20-minute multimedia show in a small amphitheater beneath the reception hall traces the history of ancient Mexico and provides a good introduction to the museum. There is a special orientation room for children, too, and an excellent shop. The exhibition halls begin on the right and deal with the origins of the earlier settlers and the pre-Classic period up to about 700 B.C. The rooms are then devoted to specific groups and their sites – the Teotihuacán pyramid-builders, the Toltecs with one of their characteristic warrior-shaped temple columns, and in the great central hall, the Mexica, or Aztecs.

The Aztec hall is dominated by the huge, intricately carved Calendar Stone, discovered in 1790 under the Zócalo. In its center is the sun. Symbols represent the 18 months of 20 days, plus five "unlucky" days, of the Aztec year. Rosettes mark the 52-year intervals initiating a new cycle, when temples were rebuilt or dedicated. A particularly frightening statue of the earth goddess Coatlicue, with a serpent head and necklace of severed hands and heart, is offset by a poetic representation of Xochipilli, lord of music and dancing, seated with legs crossed and face uplifted. Look for Moctezuma's iridescent feather headdress, a copy of the original sent by Cortés to Charles V.

Next comes the Oaxaca room, with the Mixtec breastplate of gold, silver, and turquoise and a reproduction of a Monte Albán tomb. The Gulf of Mexico room is noteworthy for its Olmec sculpture. Look for the outstanding small figure of a bearded man known as "El Luchador," the wrestler. Here are beautifully carved jade objects from the ritual ball game called *yugos* (yokes) *y hachas* (axes), the immense helmeted Olmec heads, and a superb Huastec figure of a youth with his body "tattooed" by bas-reliefs. The Maya room is equally fine. Among its many treasures are small terracotta figurines from Jaina near Campeche showing the costumes of Maya personages in minute detail; two magnificent portrait busts from Palenque; and stone stelae bearing reliefs of ceremonial scenes and Mayan hieroglyphics from Yaxchilán in the Chiapas rainforest. The remaining hall is dedicated to the appealing primitive art of northern and western Mexico.

Immediately above these halls, the upstairs museum illustrates the daily life of the descendants of each of these ancient peoples, or at least of the Indian communities now living in the same areas – Mayas above Mayas, Zapotecs, and Mixtecs above the Oaxaca hall, and so on. It is best to begin above the entrance and work around the courtyard counterclockwise, for the first room offers an introduction to the materials and methods of ethnology, the study of races. The costumes and handicrafts of each tribe and photographs of their present-day environments are exhibited with life-size models of family groups. The best view of the court and the suspended roof is from the gallery above the Mexica hall.

The courtyard arrangement makes it easy to step outside at any point and find a bench for a little rest. Here you can read on the walls Spanish translations of Aztec poetry, surprisingly sensitive for a warrior race. There is a pleasant restaurant on the garden level. Ideally, however, you shouldn't try to take in the whole museum in one visit. As in virtually all Mexican museums, explanations are only in Spanish.

Two other collections close to the entrance to the Reforma as it enters Bosque de Chapultepec are worth a visit if you are not pressed for time. The **Museo de Arte Moderno** exhibits Mexican painting and sculpture from the turn of the century to the present. The **Museo Rufino Tamayo** is less a place to view this painter's work than another example of Mexican creativity in architecture. It includes Tamayo's collection of contemporary art from other countries. Tamayo, one of Mexico's greatest 20th century artists, died of pneumonia in June 1991.

South along Insurgentes

About midway along the Reforma between the Alameda and Bosque de Chapultepec (as the venue skirts the Zona Rosa), you come to the broad Avenida Insurgentes Sur, another major thoroughfare, this one leading to many of the attractions on the south side of the capital. The first stop, a few blocks south of Reforma, is the Insurgentes Metro Station. This sunken circle shows how a necessary facility can be turned into a community asset. The plaza has shops, restaurants, book fairs, art exhibits, and sometimes concerts.

Seeing red: matador and bull face off at the world's largest bullring, the Plaza México.

Farther south, on the right at Calle Filadelfia, next to the World Trade Center, an explosion of color announces the **Polyforum Siqueiros**, a crown-shaped arts center covered with David Alfaro Siqueiros's passionate images. Inside, an auditorium houses the artist's immense three-dimensional mural, *The March of Humanity toward the Cosmos,* which you view from a moving platform. The 12-sided structure contains a theater, café, exhibition galleries, and a collection of works by the artist.

To the right of the next roundabout is the **Plaza México** – the world's largest bullring with 50,000 seats. The high season, from

Of Historical and Architectural Interest

Casa de los Azulejos *Eje Central and Madero, Centro Histórico.* Sanborn's restaurant and gift shop, open daily between 7am and 1am. Metro Bellas Artes.

Castillo de Chapultepec *Bosque de Chapultepec.* Museo Nacional de Historia open Tuesday–Sunday 10am–5pm; admission 35 pesos. Metro Chapultepec.

Colegio de San Ildefonso *Justo Sierra 16, Centro Histórico.* This former public preparatory school showcases Mexican mural art of the 20th century and is the site of major exhibits, open Daily 11am–5.30pm. Metro Zócalo.

Departamento del Distrito Federal *Pino Suárez and 16 de Septiembre, Centro Histórico.* Mexico City's City Hall. Open Monday–Friday 10am–7pm. Metro Zócalo.

Hospital de Jesús *20 de Noviembre Pasaje 82, Centro Histórico.* The first hospital in the Americas, founded by Hernán Cortés in 1524. Open Monday–Friday 9am–4pm, Saturday 9am–1pm; free admission. Metro Pino Suárez.

Monumento a la Revolución *Plaza de la Revolución.* Open Tuesday–Sunday 9am–5pm; free admission. Metro Revolución.

Palacio de Bellas Artes *Eje Central and 5 de Mayo, Centro Histórico.* Building and exhibits open to view daily 11am–7pm, when performances are not in progress. Metro Bellas Artes.

Palacio de Iturbide *Madero 17, Centro Histórico.* Open daily 10am–7pm. Metro Bellas Artes.

Palacio Nacional *Pino Suárez across from the zócalo, Centro Histórico.* Open daily 10am–6pm. Metro Zócalo.

Polyforum Cultural Siqueiros *Insurgentes Sur and Filadelfia Col. Napoles; Tel. (55) 5536-4520.* Theater opens daily to view building 10am–6pm; 15 pesos. Light and sound show for the mural Saturday and Sunday takes place at 10am, noon, and 1.30pm; admission 30 pesos. Metro Insurgentes.

Secretaría de Educación Pública *República de Cuba and República de Brasil, Centro Histórico.* Public education government offices (decorated with Diego Rivera murals) open Monday–Friday 10am–5pm. Metro Allende.

Torre Latino-Americana *Eje Central and Madero, Centro Histórico.* Open for panoramic view daily 9.30am–11pm; admission 40 pesos. Metro Bellas Artes.

October to March, takes place during the off-season in Spain, so the world's top matadors are seen here. From June or July to September apprentice bullfighters (*novilleros*) take over to fight younger, smaller bulls (*novillos*) and the Sunday afternoon card is billed as a Novillada instead of a Corrida de Toros. The posters look the same, so be alert for the wording. Novilladas can be thrilling – after all, every matador has passed this way – but they can be quite dismal, too. At least the tickets are cheaper. Many travel agencies include a bullfight in their Mexico City tours, which is a convenient way to get a ticket – you'll have a good seat along with transportation to and from the ring. (Cabs are hard to find around the Plaza México after a bullfight.)

Farther down the Insurgentes Sur, still on the right, look for Diego Rivera's mosaic on the Teatro de los Insurgentes. Even here, Rivera is preaching politics. Insurgentes next crosses into the suburb of **San Ángel**, once a village that the viceroys and elite of colonial Mexico favored for their country houses. The metropolis has grown around and beyond the village and its surrounding orchards, leaving San Ángel a village within the city, an island of narrow, cobblestone, up-and-down streets, attractive villas behind high walls, and luxury

A tranquil restaurant terrace in the Mexico City suburb of San Ángel.

boutiques. Colectivos to San Ángel run regularly from the Chapultepec metro station. They – or your taxi – can drop you off on Insurgentes Sur across the avenue from the **Iglesia y Convento de El
Carmen** (the Church and Convent of El Carmen). The rooms of the
convent are furnished with colonial antiques. Note the lovely tile
washbasins; less enchanting are the mummified nuns and priests
exposed in the crypt.

From the convent it is a short walk up to the Plaza de San Jacinto.
At number 23, there is a memorial tablet to Captain John O'Reilly and
70 ill-advised Irish members of the US Army's St. Patrick Battalion
who deserted General Scott's forces in 1847 to fight for Mexico. They

were captured and hanged in this square. Among the Sheehans and Kellys note the unexpected name of one Herman Schmidt.

San Ángel is most fun to visit on a Saturday when the **Bazar del Sábado** on the Plaza de San Jacinto and a nearby *tianguis* (street market) are in full swing. The Bazaar, open only on Saturday, is a collection of superior handicraft, jewelry, and dress shops tucked into corners around the courtyard of an old house. A buffet lunch is served in the patio, where musicians and fountains play. A pleasant walk up shady lanes brings you to the San Ángel Inn, probably the only restaurant in the world with its own chapel. It occupies the main building and gardens of a historic hacienda. (You can go in for a look or a drink without dining.) Across the street is the former home of Diego Rivera, now the **Museo Estudio Diego Rivera** (Diego Rivera Studio Museum). Among the collections are the papier maché skeletons and dolls that fascinated the prolific Mexican artist.

> When asking for directions, you might hear the words *derecho* (straight), *derecha* (right), or *izquierdo* (left).

A little farther along, and turning east where Jose María Rico intersects with Insurgentes Sur, you come to **Coyoacán** (Place of Coyotes, in Náhuatl), more accessible and less manicured than San Ángel. This neighborhood has the atmosphere of an artist's colony – there are bookshops serving coffee, sidewalk cafés, a bandstand in the zócalo that looks like a carousel without the horses, and a number of interesting crafts shops near the 1583 Iglesia de San Juan Bautista. Cortés lived here following the fall of Tenochtitlán, while the unhealthy ruins were being cleared of the dead and debris. His first wife died in the old Casa de la Malinche on Calle Higuera soon after her arrival from Cuba. Cortés was rumored to have murdered her in order to be with his Indian mistress.

A few blocks from the center of Coyoacán, you'll find the **Museo Frida Kahlo** behind a blue wall at Calle Londres 247, in the house that Diego Rivera shared with her. Her introspective canvases and self-portraits are full of the suffering she endured after a crippling accident. Her unforgettable image also appears in many of Rivera's murals. It's an interesting, idiosyncratic museum. Look for her collection of primitive *retablos* – one illustrates the escape of a grateful man who was cut down after being hanged. Nearby at Calle Viena 45 is the fortified **house of Leon Trotsky**, now a museum where his books, piles of clippings, and a Russian typewriter are preserved just as he left them. The efforts this outcast Communist took to find safe refuge in Mexico were unavailing; an agent of Stalin split Trotsky's skull with an ice pick in 1940. He is buried in the garden.

Diego Rivera's personal collection of pre-Conquest art is in the **Anahuacalli**, a pseudo-temple on the outskirts of Coyoacán, built of black lava and designed by the artist. It is best visited by taxi or tour bus, since other transportation is scarce. Among the treasures here are clay figurines with rings in their large noses from the west coast Nayarit people and a wonderfully alert, striped terracotta Colima dog once placed in a tomb to guide his dead master to the underworld.

Beyond San Ángel and Coyacán, Insurgentes Sur enters the Pedregal, a vast sheet of lava more than 3 m (10 ft) thick, now covered by a residential district and the **Ciudad Universitaria**, the campus of the national university of Mexico. The lava flowed from a small volcano around 450 B.C. when the site was already inhabited. While quarrying building stone here at the turn of the century, engineers discovered skeletons and artifacts dating back to 1100 B.C. Some of these may be seen in tunnels in the lava at Copilco, an archeological site off the avenue to the left.

The Ciudad Universitaria was founded in 1551 and is the oldest in the Americas, while its campus is one of the most modern. The complex, opened in 1954, shows why contemporary Mexican architecture has admirers worldwide. The ten-story block on stilts encrusted with mosaics is the central library, designed by artist Juan O'Gorman. Murals and mosaics decorate almost every building. One of the most striking is the three-dimensional Siqueiros mural on the rectory, designed to be observed from cars moving along Insurgentes. Rivera's contribution is on the other side of the avenue, stone reliefs of Mexican sports from past and present on the Olympic Stadium.

The Feathered Serpent

Ancient Mexicans ranked their gods in terms of local needs: where crops depended on uncertain rainfall, the rain god was supreme; where sunshine was unreliable, the sun god took precedence. Quetzalcóatl, the Feathered Serpent and God of the Morning Star, the Wind, and the Arts, was different. He was a more universal deity, perhaps introduced by the people of Teotihuacán and exalted by the Toltecs. According to legend, he created man with his own blood, then turned himself into an ant in order to steal a grain of maize from the ants. He gave this most important life-sustaining gift to men, and did not require human sacrifices in return.

Around 968 a Toltec king named Ce Acatl Topiltzín also served as a priest of Quetzalcóatl in Tollan (Tula). He was fair-skinned and had a beard, which is unusual among the Indian race. Topiltzín was a peaceful ruler, but he fell afoul of a warlike brother and was forced to leave Tollan. To the confusion of scholars, this genuine historical figure entered legend as a demi-god, also called Quetzalcóatl. It is told that he moved east, as far as the land of the Maya. The Maya venerated him as Kukulcán, meaning "feathered serpent" in their tongue. It is obvious from many features of Chichén Itzá and other cities that Toltec influence was present at about that time.

Topiltzín-Quetzalcóatl-Kukulcán moved on. He is said to have sailed toward the east on a serpent raft, promising to return. And so, four centuries later, when Moctezuma learned that bearded men sailing on "floating houses" had arrived in his dominions, he was sure the god had kept his promise. He greeted Cortés as the returning deity, welcomed the Spanish forces into his capital, and opened the way to the Conquest.

There's one more sight to see on Insurgentes. The eruption that buried Copilco also covered Mexico's oldest complete pyramid, **Cuicuilco**, which you come upon at the spot where the avenue crosses the Periférico. The structure – three concentric rings of baked clay and stone – had apparently been abandoned for centuries before being swallowed up by lava. A small museum displays objects found on the site and explains the origins of the Pedregal.

Xochimilco

Follow the Periférico ring road east from Insurgentes past the Ciudad Universitaria to reach **Xochimilco** and its famous **Floating Gardens**. All tour companies include a trip here. It can also be reached in about an hour by a combination of Metro line 2 to Taxqueña and colectivo 36 from the station, for a round-trip cost of about 10 pesos.

In Aztec times, flowers, trees, and vegetables were planted on artificial rafts of mud and reeds set afloat in Lago Texcoco. Eventually, these *chinampas* became anchored as roots reached the lake bottom. Indian market gardeners ferried their produce in canoes to sell on the canals of Tenochtitlán. Nowadays the gardens have blossomed into a sort of Mexican Venice: on flower-bedecked barges, boatmen pole festive groups or romantic couples through tree-lined waterways. Mariachi musicians on the docks board the barges or cruise the canals on boats of their own, coming alongside to play requests. Photographers implore passengers to immortalize the moment by posing beneath the floral arch with the barge's name – *Conchita* and *Lupita* seem to be favorites.

Time and growth have not been kind to Xochimilco. The town is still devoted to gardening and there is a marvelous flower market in the center, where you can buy carved, painted canes and fresh fruit as well. But the canals are green with pollution, and the bottleneck of taxis and buses around the plaza on Sundays seems to have taken root like the chinampas. It is not a tourist trap, however – most of the crowd is Mexican, many in family groups with picnics, and the

Detail and full view of the Sun Pyramid of Teotihuacán as seen from the Pyramid of the Moon.

music, hurly-burly, and general commotion are authentic. Nearby, on the grounds of a former hacienda, is the **Museo Dolores Olmedo,** which showcases an outstanding collection of paintings by Diego Rivera and Frida Kahlo.

AROUND THE CAPITAL
☞ The Pyramids of Teotihuacán

North of Mexico City, Teotihuacán and its pyramids are both awesome and awe-inspiring. The city was built on an impressive scale two thousand years ago by an unknown race, and had been in ruins

for more than 600 years when the Aztecs rediscovered it and called it "the place where gods were born," reflecting the Aztec's belief that the universe was created here.

This was the first great city of the western hemisphere, with a population of more than 200,000 and an area of 11 sq km (7 sq miles). At its zenith around A.D. 500, the city counted more inhabitants than contemporary Rome could. Its style and symbols were copied by the Toltecs and Aztecs. It was a place of pilgrimage and trade, as evidenced by objects from all over Mexico found in its ruins. But it had no fortifications and presumably never recovered from an attack by barbarians who sacked and burned it around

A.D. 700. By the 16th century the city had become so covered by earth and vegetation that the Spaniards marched past without even seeing it.

Teotihuacán is just over an hour's drive north of Mexico City. To travel here, exit the city on the northern end of Insurgentes and follow the highway to Pachuca, past the first toll booth, where the exit to Teotihuacán is clearly marked. Buses depart every two hours from the Indios Verdes metro terminal, and other buses depart from the Central Norte de Autobuses for San Juan Teotihuacán. Buses cost 22 to 35 pesos, depending on the line. You can also hire a private taxi, paying an hourly rate of approximately 90 pesos. The driver, who can generally double as a private guide, will take you here, wait for you, and drive you back, generally making for a full six- to eight-hour day.

At the entrance, a state-of-the-art museum with interactive exhibits provides an introduction to the site. Opened in 1995, it has, in one part, a glass floor on which visitors walk above models of the pyramids. Nearby, a small but exceptional bookstore offers a wide selection of books in various languages on Mexican history and archaeology. The museum opens on to the 39-m (130-ft) wide **Calzada de los Muertos** (Street of the Dead), the broad esplanade that ran 4 km (2½ miles) from the Pirámide de la Luna (Pyramid of the Moon) at the north end to a still unexcavated point to the south. Straight ahead at the avenue's midpoint is the Ciudadela (citadel), a walled quadrangle with the **Templo de Quetzalcóatl** (Temple of the Feathered Serpent) at the rear, along with a dozen ceremonial platforms on four sides. (A small pyramid covers part of an earlier temple to the god; you can enter it from the right.) A staircase is flanked by heads of a serpent, whose body wriggles along the base. Framed heads of the white-fanged deity and of the round-eyed rain god Tláloc as well as conch-shell designs cover the walls.

The Calzada de los Muertos is lined with stone temple foundations, all formed by a sloping skirt (*talud*) surmounted by a boxed mural panel (*tablero*), the characteristic elements of Teotihuacán architecture.

In the time of the Aztecs, these monuments were earth-covered mounds thought to be tombs – hence the street's misleading name. It is, in fact, the grand aisle of an open-air cathedral, big enough to accommodate the scores of thousands who thronged here on sacred days.

The Pirámide del Sol (Pyramid of the Sun), on the right, served as the altar, rising 64½ m (215 ft) on a base that is 221 m (738 ft) long on each side. Stand at the foot of the stairs and imagine the wonderment of the crowds looking up to the priests at the summit chanting to trumpets and drums. The sheer mass of the pyramid is overwhelming. It is composed of an estimated 3.5 million tons of mud brick and stone, raised around A.D. 100 by a workforce of thousands without the benefit of metal tools, work animals, or the wheel. Originally, the pyramid and most of the other monuments of Teotihuacán were covered with a thick layer of plaster. You can see from bits here and there that much of it was painted red. In this and other reconstructed archaeological sites throughout Mexico, the restored sections are indicated by a regular peppering of small stones in the cement. The 247 steps to the top are easier going up than coming down, because the steep pitch can easily instill a sense of vertigo. Persistent sellers of flutes and "genuine" clay idols stake out the places where climbers stop to rest. But the effort is rewarded by a sweeping view of the orderly plan and grandeur of Teotihuacán. Behind the pyramid and south of the citadel are the geometrical grassy lumps that outline miles of still unexcavated sections of the city. On the summit platform a wood-and-thatch temple originally stood. The pyramid was built on top of a 300 B.C. shrine and cave, which was thought to be the birthplace of the sun.

The **Pirámide de la Luna** (Pyramid of the Moon) stands in its own plaza at the end of the ceremonial avenue. The moon pyramid is 45 m (152 ft) high, but since it is built on a rise, its summit is roughly even with that of the **Pirámide del Sol**. A number of palatial residences of priests or nobles have been discovered nearby. The **Palacio del Quetzalpapálotl** to the west has two elegant courtyards reached by a stair surmounted by a giant serpent's head. Carved reliefs on the columns of the lower patio represent a bird, the quetzal, and a butterfly, whose Náhuatl name, *papálotl*, is curiously like the French *papillon* and Italian *papavero*. Discs of obsidian filled the now-vacant eyeholes and traces of red, green, and blue coloring can be seen. The whole city must have glowed.

Teotihuacán is remarkable for its well-preserved murals. Jaguars adorn the walls of the **Palacio de los Jaguares** (Jaguar Palace), and the **Templo de Caracoles Emplumados** (Temple of the Feathered Shells) is decorated with parrots and conches. The most lively and extensive paintings are in the Tepantitla complex near the parking lot behind the Pirámide del Sol. In one scene, swimmers frolic in a lake. Another shows ball players with blue bats. The ruins of Teotihuacán are open daily 8am–5pm. Admission Monday–Saturday is 35 pesos; free on Sunday. There is a fee of 25 pesos for use of a video camera.

If you return to Mexico City on Highway 132D, you can make the short detour to **Acolman** to see the early Augustinian monastery, now a museum. Whenever you see a major church out in the middle of nowhere, you can bet that it was the site of an important Aztec temple. The monks first destroyed the heathen shrine, then replaced it with their own. This one is a good example of a church-fortress, built when the Indians were still considered a threat. It has medieval crenellation on the roof and a strong protective wall around the buildings. The cells and cloister still reflect the austerity of monastic life.

☛ Puebla

The trip to Puebla, southeast of Mexico City, makes a memorable day's outing. Highway 190 from Mexico City climbs to 3,000 m (10,000 ft) through pines and upland meadows and descends through apple orchards, where you can stop to buy cider. Along the way, you get great close-up views of Popocatépetl and Iztaccíhuatl volcanoes. All of Puebla is a national historical monument noted for its large historical center containing many convents, churches, and colonial mansions. The city receives many visitors, who come to see the sights

*Marvel at the ornate Indian Baroque interior of the
Tonantzintla Church, just outside Puebla.*

and enjoy some of the food for which Puebla is famous, including
such dishes as *mole poblano* (a rich sauce, poured over turkey or
chicken, that contains more than 30 ingredients, including three kinds
of chiles, chocolate, and nuts) and *chile relleno en nogada* (a poblano
chile that has been peeled and stuffed with a mixture of pork, chicken,

nuts, and raisins and covered in a walnut cream sauce topped with pomegranate seeds). These and other dishes were invented by nuns here during colonial times.

Another tradition in Puebla is a centuries-old ceramics craft called *talavera,* known for the polycromatic designs with a predominance of blue, yellow, and orange. Talavera dinnerware and *azulejos* (tiles) are expensive but very popular. You will see the azulejos made in the Talavera style all over Puebla on colonial façades, church domes, and interiors, setting Puebla apart from all other colonial cities in Mexico.

The **cathedral** in Puebla is Mexico's second largest. It overlooks a shady zócalo lined with shops and cafés beneath the colonial arcades. To its left, on Avenida 5 Oriente, the **Biblioteca Palafoxiana** (Palafoxiana Library) in the former archbishop's palace contains interesting maps and manuscripts amid intricate paneling. Across the zócalo and two blocks down the pedestrians-only Calle 5 de Mayo, the church of Santo Domingo's **Capilla del Rosario** (Rosary Chapel) is Mexican Churrigueresque at its most dazzling. Every centimeter of this 17th-century jewel-box masterpiece is worked in gold-covered wood and plaster set off by a white stucco background. Wildly ornate carvings of cherubs and saints are lost in the foliage of a gold jungle.

Three blocks east of Santo Domingo is the **Mercado Parián,** a market of small shops selling onyx, embroidery, and ceramics. Adjoining this market is the Barrio del Artista, a cobblestone street two blocks long bordered by a number of art galleries. Two other destinations in downtown Puebla are most entertaining. One is the **Museo Amparo**, the largest museum downtown, exhibiting a collection of pre-Columbian and colonial art. The other is the "hidden convent" on Avenida 18 Poniente, which operated clandestinely from 1857 to 1934 after it was supposedly closed by the anticlerical Reform Laws. Entry was through a concealed door in an adjoining house that led to two small cloisters and an upstairs gallery, where the nuns could peek into a church below. Policemen in the stationhouse next door must have been in on the secret – or singularly unobservant. The most interesting room is the kitchen, with a circular tile stove of delicate, blue and white stars and flowers.

Ten minutes outside of Puebla, on the old highway 190 to Mexico City, is the town of **Cholula**, a very important religious center in Pre-Columbian times. In downtown Cholula, you'll find the largest pyramid by volume in the world. It remains unreconstructed and covered in vegetation. At first glimpse, you might think it a small hill, but if you climb the pyramid in front (also unreconstructed) you will see clearly the outlines of a large four-tiered structure. There was a fifth tier, but the Spaniards replaced it with a church – Nuestra Señora de los Remedios. You can also walk through tunnels dug by archeologists to explore the earlier stages of the pyramid's construction.

The pyramid was surrounded by hundreds of smaller pyramids, according to Cortés. On his march to Tenochtitlán he forestalled an ambush here by slaughtering thousands of the population and burning the temples. These were later covered by churches – there was supposed to be

> Before asking a question or making a request of someone, always begin with a greeting: *buenos días* (good morning), *buenas tardes* (good afternoon), or *buenas noches* (good evening).

one for every day of the year. This may once have been true, but now there are 47, which is quite enough for a town of 20,000.

Just to the south of Cholula are two more churches, which are famous for their beauty: Tonantzintla, with its impressive Indian Baroque interior, which the writer R. Gordon Wasson interpreted as having several allusions to a secret native mushroom cult, and San Francisco de Acatepec, with its brightly colored tile façade.

Cuernavaca and Taxco

Over the mountains south of Mexico City, **Cuernavaca** luxuriates in a setting drenched in color. Blossoming flame trees, bougainvillea, hibiscus, camellias, and poinsettia blaze along streets where jacarandas

stand in blue pools of fallen petals. Because of the year-round spring climate, the rich and famous long ago picked the city for their winter homes – their red-roofed villas are hidden behind high walls. The 60-minute drive from the capital is along the toll expressway, Highway 95, which is also the fastest route to Taxco (pronounced Tahss-co) and Acapulco, respectively two hours and 3½ hours from Mexico City (see pages 78 and 112). A parallel, prettier non-toll road, 95D, follows the same path as 95. Buses from Mexico City leave for Cuernavaca every half hour from the Terminal de Autobuses del Sur, near Taxqueña.

As you approach the town, you climb through pinewoods and meadows, then drop to a 1,665 m (5,460 ft) plateau from which Cuernavaca looks out over the lush Morelos Valley and back at the snow-capped volcanoes. All the land stretching as far as the eye can see was once part of the domain granted to Cortés when he was given the title Marquis del Valle de Oaxaca by King Charles V. After tearing down an Aztec pyramid temple for stone, the old campaigner built a fortress-palace for himself around 1530. He introduced sheep, cattle, the silkworm, and Cuban sugar cane, still extensively grown in the valley. The palace is now the **Museo de Cuauhnáhuac** – the Aztec name for the town ("place at the edge of the forest"), distorted by the Spaniards to Cuernavaca ("cow's horn"). There are cultural and historical exhibits, including relics of the original inhabitants. A highlight of the museum is a Diego Rivera mural of the valley's history, commissioned in 1928 by US Ambassador Dwight Morrow as a gift to Mexico. It depicts the conquerors lolling in hammocks while natives tote sugar cane, and repeats the often-painted scene of Spaniards burning Cuauhtémoc's feet in the vain attempt to force him to reveal the location of Moctezuma's treasure. Emiliano Zapata, the revolutionary hero who became famous for his battle cry of "*tierra y libertad*" ("land and liberty"), appears on his white horse.

Floral fantasy...Float away into an exotic world on a flower-bedecked barge in Xochimilco, the "Mexican Venice."

The **cathedral** is set back from the bustle of the streets in a park-like corner. The crenellations on the roof proclaim it to be from the early 16th century, when churches doubled as strongholds. The interior is a surprise – under the old barrel vault, the altar is an abstract modern construction, lit by sunbeams from high windows. Unconventional, too, is the rousing "Mariachi mass," held every Sunday and accompanied by mariachi music, the traditional music of Mexico, rather than the more traditional organ music. A refurbishing of the nave in 1967 uncovered 17th-century frescoes showing the martyrdom of St. Felipe de Jesús, crucified in 1597 in Nagasaki with 25 Franciscan missionaries. Across a courtyard, the Baroque façade of the **Capilla de la Tercera Orden** has the added charm of being adorned with naïve designs showing Indian men dancing, a reminder that Indian labor built these churches. The altar's retablo, the gilded, carved wooden screen, is notable. A band of blue Talavera tile from Puebla around the walls enhances this attractive chapel.

A short walk up the Avenida Morelos leads to the **Casa Borda** and the **Jardín Borda**. Once the magnificent villa of an 18th-century silver magnate, it was taken over by Emperor Maximilian as his private preserve in the mid-1800s, when it served as the setting for his romantic interludes with his lover, La India Bonita. The botanical gardens, complete with kiosks and an artificial lake, continue to flourish, and the front rooms house an art center, Centro de Arte Jardín Borda. The gardens are a frequent venue for concerts and art exhibits.

Cuernavaca has suffered in recent years – industrial development clouds the once-clear air, traffic clogs the downtown streets, and the three connected plazas of the zócalo with their sidewalk cafés have become somewhat of a crowded bazaar. The old street market has been moved across the ravine that divides the city, a short walk behind and to the left of the Museo de Cuauhnáhuac. Although confined to an enclosure, the market is nevertheless bursting with vitality and overflowing with exotic produce, including an assortment of powders, leaves, bottled snakes, and bark and roots guaranteed to cure everything from phlebitis to impotency. More of the same may be examined in the **Museo de Medicina Tradicional**, in a house at 200 Calle Matamoros called "la Casa del Olvido" ("House of Forgetfulness"), also said to have been used by Maximilian for trysts with his Mexican mistress.

A short taxi ride brings you to the **Pirámide de Teopanzolco**, still within the city. From its top you can look down on to an earlier pyramid inside, covered by the outer structure. Until 1910 the mound was thought to be a hill, but when the rebel Zapata put some guns here and their recoil dug into the thin topsoil, the building stone beneath was revealed.

Cuernavaca is known for its Spanish-language schools. Noteworthy, too, are the spas and thermal waters in and around Cuernavaca.

> In colonial cities, you won't see stop signs at many intersections. Look instead for small signs with arrows posted on the corners of buildings. If the arrow is black, you have the right of way; if it is red, you must stop.

There are worthwhile short excursions to the attractive village of Tepoztlán and the archaeologically important hilltop ruins of Xochicalco dating from 200 B.C.

The drive to **Taxco** takes about an hour, part on highway 95 to the coast and part on a pleasant winding road. About 20 km (13 miles) before reaching Taxco, a turn-off to Toluca on the right marked "Grutas" leads to the Grutas de Cacahuamilpa, one of the most extensive cave systems in Mexico. Huge caverns 60 m (200 ft) high drip with stalactites and amazing limestone formations that run some 70 km (45 miles) underground, most still unexplored. Guided tours are daily 10am–5pm, and take about an hour and a half. Cost for the tour is 30 pesos, children under twelve 20 pesos.

The white walls, red roofs, and flower-filled balconies of Taxco spill down a green hillside. The blue-and-yellow dome and twin pink spires of **Iglesia de Santa Prisca** provide the centerpiece of this picture-postcard scene, a long-time favorite with tourists. The whole town is a national monument. It was founded by Cortés to exploit Indian silver mines, but the richest desposits were discovered in the 18th century by José de la Borda. He became so wealthy that he built gardens and mansions and paid for the total reconstruction of Santa Prisca, explaining that "God has given to Borda, now Borda gives to God." The church's rosy façade practically writhes with spiral columns and

twisted martyrs. Faces peer out of the stone at every angle. The ornate golden altar is worthy of this community of jewelers. You'll find their shops in every street and especially around the Plaza Borda, the sloping zócalo in front of the church.

Mines that honeycomb the hill beneath the town are still being worked – you'll hear the steam whistle when shifts change – but today the source of wealth is silver jewelry. An American, William Spratling, started it all when he came to Taxco in the 1930s, set up a silver workshop, and taught local craftsmen to use ancient designs in modern products. The **Museo Guillermo Spratling** (open Tuesday–Saturday, 10am–5pm), just below the square,

All that glitters...Taxco's silver treasures and stunning hilltop location continue to bewitch.

holds the American's fine collection of Pre-Columbian art and features historical exhibits as well.

The fun in Taxco is to climb up and down the narrow streets, comparing prices and bargaining, and watching artisans cutting, filing, and polishing silver, obsidian, and semi-precious stones. Take a break on a restaurant balcony overlooking the square, from which descends a

long staircase lined with market stalls and food stands where you are served from steaming clay cauldrons. On Calle John F. Kennedy at the bottom, cabs and colectivos pass continually to take you back up the hill. From the heights of Monte Taxco, reached by a cable car, there's a great view over the town. Find a seat at sunset on one of the hotel terraces on the slopes overlooking Taxco to watch the sky turn pink behind Santa Prisca and the lights of the town spark like fireflies.

SILVER CITIES

For colonial atmosphere, the "Silver Cities" are pure gold. The Spaniards never found the legendary city of El Dorado, but they did discover ore in the mountains northwest of Mexico City that poured out a river of silver for centuries and continue to make Mexico *numero uno* in world production. Through-

> **The word for parking lot is *estacionamiento*. Cede el paso is "yield," and *alto* is "stop."**

out the 17th and 18th centuries, while Indians slaved in the mines, immensely rich mine-owners lavished fortunes on handsome cities literally built on silver. They embellished them with splendid churches, public buildings, and stately mansions for themselves. But these wealthy families were mostly *criollos*, born in Mexico of Spanish descent, and as such not entitled to hold the political offices reserved for the *peninsulares*, born in Spain. Early in the 19th century, criollos plotted to throw out the royalist peninsulares and for a time they made common cause with the oppressed Indians and mestizos of the mining towns. Thus the Silver Cities are known as the "cradle of Mexican independence." Of more recent fame are the charm of their picturesque streets and the mild climate, draws for artists, retirees, and tourists alike – and with them have come attractive hostelries, shops, and restaurants.

This region is easily accessible and makes for a great introduction to interior Mexico. Most travel agencies in Mexico City offer organized tours of at least some of these cities, but a leisurely trip would

Olé!

The art of bullfighting inspires extremes: some see it as unacceptably cruel animal torture, while others esteem it as a richly symbolic drama involving grace and courage. Whatever your opinion, the *corridas de toros* are an important, even essential, element of Mexico's culture.

Beyond the opening procession, the corrida follows a fixed pattern and is divided into three parts, or *tercios*. The first tercio begins when the gate is banged open and the bull charges out into the ring. The fans and the matador watch carefully to see if the animal has the size, speed, and fury required of a *toro bravo*. The matador impresses the fans with elaborate cape work in long sequences that, if done with grace and courage, will produce enthusiastic "ole's" from the public. In the second tercio, the matador or one of his assistants will place *banderillas* (steel barbs on decorated sticks) into the hump of the bull's neck muscle to allow the bull to bleed so that he won't become congested and run out of strength before the fight is over.

In the final, fatal tercio, the matador exchanges his cape for the *muleta*, a red cloth draped over a sword; he demonstrates his control and his courage with a series of passes. This is where he is very likely to be gored, as most matadors eventually are. If the bull is a brave one, and if the matador is at the same time courageous, graceful, and working close to the horns, the crowd may demand music and the "olés!" may rock the bullring. The end comes when the matador takes another sword and salutes his lady-love or whoever else he may dedicate the bull to. After a few more passes, he will "fix" the bull so that its head is down and its eyes focused on the muleta. This exposes the point on the spine where the matador aims his sword. To kill properly, he must plunge it in over the horns. If all goes well, the bull will drop dead on the spot. If the matador has performed well, the presiding official may award him the bull's ear, two ears, or – triumph! – two ears and the tail.

be far more enjoyable. From the capital there is excellent first-class bus service to any of these towns from the northern bus terminal, and a modern express toll road (Highway 57D) takes you directly to the closest of these cities, Querétaro, in three hours.

You can leave the highway just short of Querétaro to spend a pleasant hour in **San Juan del Río**, a trim, white colonial town where many shops sell opals mined from the region. Another 12 km (7½ miles) leads to **Tequisquiapan**, where hotels and public pools offer baths fed by radioactive hot springs, said to be good for arthritis. It's a popular spa, with good shops, riding, and a golf course.

Querétaro

The outskirts of Querétaro are industrial, so press on to the historic center of town and the **Plaza de Armas**, a beautiful little main square shaded by trimmed laurel trees and accessible by pedestrian-only streets. From here you can stroll in any direction and come upon stately colonial houses, exquisitely decorated Baroque churches, and expansive convents. On the plaza is the **Casa de la Corregidora** (now the city hall). Here, in 1810, lived a heroine of the War of Independence known as

The most popular of the silver cities, San Miguel de Allende, retains its quaint charm.

"la Corregidora," because, as wife of the Corregidor (city council-man), she risked her life to warn a group plotting revolt from Spain that their conspiracy had been uncovered by the government. Though locked in her room, she was still able to get a message out to the priest Miguel Hidalgo, who was to become the father of Mexico when he gave the cry for independence from his parish church in the nearby town of Dolores.

On the opposite side of the plaza is the **Casa de Ecala**, with the its impressive 18th-century Baroque façade. Down Calle Madero is the **Iglesia Santa Clara**, whose simple exterior conceals a stunning-ly complex Baroque interior. The altar screen is a masterpiece of carving and gilding. The Neptune fountain next to the church is by the great 18th-century architect Eduardo Tresguerras. A block south on Calle Allende is the former convent of San Agustín, completed in 1743 with an elaborate façade and a courtyard encrusted with sculp-tures in the late-Baroque style. Now it houses the state art museum.

The **Museo Regional**, on Calle Corregidora two blocks east of Santa Clara, occupies the magnificent former convent of the Fran-ciscans and is worth a trip just to see the building. The museum holds a large collection of historical artifacts, including many items dating from the time when Maximilian was Mexico's emperor. Maximilian's final defeat took place just outside of Querétaro, and he was executed at the nearby Cerro de las Campanas (Hill of the Bells), where you will find a small Habsburg chapel. Two blocks north of the Museo is the Teatro de la República, a grand 19th-cen-tury theater where a court met to decide Maximilian's fate.

San Miguel de Allende

San Miguel de Allende became rich as a market center for the sur-rounding mining communities. The town of some 50,000 is special because it has kept its original appearance intact. It is the smallest and most relaxing of the silver cities. You come upon it from above and can look down on spires of pink stone, domes of bright majolica,

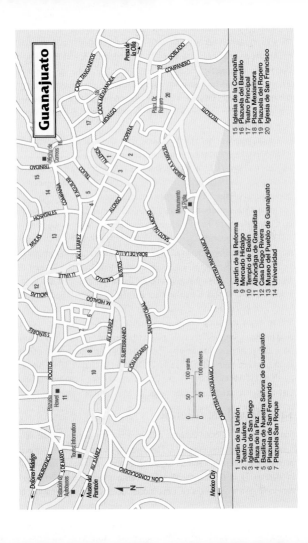

Guanajuato

1 Jardin de la Unión
2 Teatro Juárez
3 Iglesia de San Diego
4 Plaza de la Paz
5 Basílica de Nuestra Señora de Guanajuato
6 Plazuela de San Fernando
7 Plazuela San Roque

8 Jardín de la Reforma
9 Mercado Hidalgo
10 Templo de Belén
11 Alhóndiga de Granaditas
12 Casa Diego Rivera
13 Museo del Pueblo de Guanajuato
14 Universidad

15 Iglesia de la Compañía
16 Plazuela del Baratillo
17 Teatro Principal
18 Plaza Mexiamora
19 Plazuela del Ropero
20 Iglesia de San Francisco

white walls, and red roof tiles. The whole, perfect ensemble is protected as a national monument. Cobblestone streets descend to the main square, called simply "El Jardín," and a most unexpected 1880s Gothic-inspired church. **La Parroquia** is the work of a local mason and 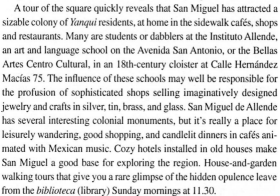 architect, Zeferino Gutiérrez, who took his inspiration from a postcard image of a French cathedral. It is a great source of pride for residents.

A tour of the square quickly reveals that San Miguel has attracted a sizable colony of *Yanqui* residents, at home in the sidewalk cafés, shops and restaurants. Many are students or dabblers at the Instituto Allende, an art and language school on the Avenida San Antonio, or the Bellas Artes Centro Cultural, in an 18th-century cloister at Calle Hernández Macías 75. The influence of these schools may well be responsible for the profusion of sophisticated shops selling imaginatively designed jewelry and crafts in silver, tin, brass, and glass. San Miguel de Allende has several interesting colonial monuments, but it's really a place for leisurely wandering, good shopping, and candlelit dinners in cafés animated with Mexican music. Cozy hotels installed in old houses make San Miguel a good base for exploring the region. House-and-garden walking tours that give you a rare glimpse of the hidden opulence leave from the *biblioteca* (library) Sunday mornings at 11.30.

Don't miss the **Oratorio**, a church built on a platform above the market and housing the tombs of the Conde de la Canal and his wife. The Canal family built grand houses in the town, but San Miguel's most famous son is Ignacio Allende, one of the heroes of the 1810 uprising for independence. San Miguel's name was extended to honor him. His house, just off the Jardín on Calle Cuna de Allende, is a museum furnished in period style.

Guanajuato

Guanajuato is capital of the state of the same name. The 90-minute drive west from San Miguel de Allende passes through the rolling plains of the fertile Bajío district. Guanajuato is tucked deep in the folds of a river gorge encircled by rounded hills. The topography defeats the grid pattern of most Mexican towns. Streets and alleys tumble down steep slopes and twist about among small irregular plazas. The houses, conforming to the hillsides they are built on, seem to have been thrown together in a jumble and are painted in softly glowing shades. Almost all have balconies overflowing with flowers, and there's a competition in May for the prettiest.

Driving in town is hopeless; park in a hillside garage above the **Jardín de la Unión**, the hub of the city. Laurel trees grow entwined to shade this small plaza. Side-by-side across the street are the **Teatro Juárez**, a 1903 extravaganza in the French style dear to the dictator Porfirio Díaz, and the delicately decorated 18th-century pink stone San Diego church. Following this street leads up to the Plaza de la Paz, hemmed in by imposing mansions and the **Basílica de Nuestra Señora de Guanajuato**, one of the city's most impressive colonial monuments. The interior is neoclassic, with huge chandeliers and an altar to the Virgin, whose image was given by King Philip II of Spain. It stands, like the city, on a base of silver. Behind the church, the University of Guanajuato's white Moorish front looks old, but isn't. Next door is La Compañía, the church of the Jesuits who founded the university. The façade is one of the earliest examples of Mexican Baroque.

On the other side of the university, Calle Pocitos leads to the **Museo del Pueblo de Guanajuato**, lodged in the palace of the Marqués de Rayas. The museum is mainly devoted to religious paintings. A more interesting landmark a bit farther down the street at number 67 is the house where Diego Rivera was born, in 1896. His evolution from these bourgeois beginnings into a revolutionary painter is documented in a small museum upstairs. Follow the street's ups and downs to the **Alhóndiga de Granaditas**. Guanajuato's royalists took refuge in this fortress-like granary in 1810 when the city was attacked by the undisciplined peasant army led by Father Hidalgo. When entrance to the fortress was finally gained, Father Hidalgo lost control of his peasant soldiers, who rushed in

Tales from the crypt: Mum's the word from the cadavers at the Museo del Panteón, Guanajuato.

and hacked to death many of the people inside. The massacre hurt the movement's chances for success by alienating many from the cause, and grieved Hidalgo sorely. When the tide later turned, the royalists took revenge by placing the heads of Hidalgo, Allende, and two other independence leaders in small iron cages suspended from the four corners of the granary. The Alhóndiga is both a shrine to independence and a good museum featuring pre-Columbian artifacts, regional crafts and costumes.

A block below, in the broad Hidalgo market you can get a good look at the different foodstuffs, garnishes, and condiments that locals use in their cooking, including *tomatillos* (little green fruit with a papery skin used in sauces), brown tamarind pods, nopales, cactus paddles, mamey fruit, several kinds of avocados, the creased green and spiny *chayote* (the "vegetable pear" that tastes like a delicate squash), fresh cilantro leaves, and the *epazote* herb with spiky leaves. The gray-black ears of corn you may see are deformed by *huitlacoche*, a fungus prized for making a stuffing with a spicy mushroom flavor. Bright yellow squash blossoms are chopped and fried as filling for folded, toasted tortillas called quesadillas. You can sample fruit, buy herbal remedies, eat mummy-shaped nut candy, and on the balcony above, browse through handicraft stalls.

In October and November Guanajuato hosts one of Mexico's most important cultural events, the International Cervantes Festival. It all began with traditional university student performances of short skits, or *entremeses*, by Cervantes, staged in the open air in the Plazuela San Roque off the Avenida Juarez. Now the three-week program attracts orchestras, ballets, theater groups, singers, and chamber

Not to be missed: The 18th-century stone façade of the cathedral in Zacatecas will impress even the weariest traveler.

musicians, and includes a film festival and art exhibits. Every theater, hall, church, and plaza in town is converted into performing space. Ticket and hotel reservations must be made many months in advance.

Following Avenida Juarez back toward the Jardín, you'll come to the Plazuela de los Angeles. Off this square is an alley, or rather a passage, so narrow that the flower-filled balconies almost touch. It's called the **Callejón del Beso**, the Alley of the Kiss. Guides – and any kid playing in the street becomes one at the sight of a foreigner – reel off a Romeo-and-Juliet yarn here about a rich merchant's daughter and poor boy from the mines who kissed across facing balconies.

The best views of the whole city can be taken in from a road that climbs the canyon walls and encircles the town, the **Carretera Panorámica**. On this road above the Jardín de la Unión is a stone statue of the brave El Pípila, the miner who tied a flagstone to his back for protection from enemy fire and crawled up to the door of La Alhóndiga and set it ablaze. It makes a good vantage point. The most macabre sight in Guanajuato is at the **Museo del Panteón**, the cemetery museum, on the outskirts. On display there are scores of naturally mummified cadavers propped up in glass cases. In Mexico, grave space is rented to families for fixed periods and then, unless more money is paid, the bones are exhumed and returned to the family to make room for other bodies. Because the bodies were preserved, there was little else that could be done with them.

> Bus travel between cities is inexpensive and comfortable. *Primera* (first-class) and *segunda* (second-class) bus tickets are always sold at different counters if not different bus stations.

A few kilometers out on the road to Dolores Hidalgo, the **Iglesia de la Valenciana** sits on top of what was the richest silver deposit in the world. The Valenciana mine made its owner fabulously rich and earned him a title, the Count of Valenciana. In gratitude, in 1788 he built a perfect gem of Mexican Baroque in pink stone dedicated to

San Cayetano. Note the finely carved and painted features and robes of the figures on the gilded main altar, each a little masterpiece within the whirling, exalted whole. Guanajuato's mines have produced more than a billion dollars worth of silver and are still at it. You can visit the mine and in the village find shops selling rock crystals and other minerals. Rock hounds won't want to miss the **Museo de Minería** in the school of mines on this road just above the city.

☛ Zacatecas

Zacatecas, 325 km (200 miles) north of Guanajuato, is in high, desolate terrain 2,500 m (8,200 ft) above sea level. For a panoramic view, ride the cable car up to the **Cerro de la Bufa**, a craggy hill that dominates the center of town. Looking out over the wild and barren land will make you feel like you're on the frontier. From up here you can see at least three mines – this is mining country, and Zacatecas leads Mexico in the production of silver and several other metals.

The city has the best preserved colonial historic center in Mexico, and through civic pride, Zacatecans have gone to the trouble of burying power and phone cables to unclutter the urban views. It is a sheer delight to walk the streets here. When you do, make sure you take in the façade of the **cathedral**. There is nothing like it in all of Mexico – its stone carving has so much depth and is so richly worked that no photo does it justice. Other sights worth seeing are the **Museo Rafael Coronel**, a collection of native and folk masks from all over Mexico, and the **Museo Pedro Coronel**, with wonderful art works from the world over. If you're interested in seeing what put this little town on the map, take a tour of the **El Edén mine**, an abandoned shaft almost in the middle of town. For explanations in English, you can hire a tour guide for trip around the city.

San Luis Potosí

The city of San Luis Potosí, two hours north of San Miguel, has grown more than any silver city, but you wouldn't be able to tell from the appearance of the historical center of town. There, people congregate in the many beautiful plazas and pedestrian walkways that the city is known for, much like people do in any small town in Mexico. The Churrigueresque red stone **Templo del Carmen** and the **Museo de la Máscara** (National Mask Museum), with 1,500 masks used in Indian and religious festivals from every part of Mexico, are the standout attractions.

The ghost town of **Real de Catorce**, an hour's drive to the north, was a boisterous mining community of 30,000 at the end of the 19th century. You can poke around its well-preserved ruins, empty shops, cantinas, a theater, and cock-fighting arena. Another place to go lies an hour to the east, Xilitla, where early in this century a strange Englishman constructed modern-day ruins on a mountain in the forested Huasteca region of the state.

MICHOACÁN AND JALISCO

Michoacán and Jalisco, though neighboring states, are quite different. Michoacán is a state known for its beautiful and dramatic landscapes, and for being host to millions of monarch butterflies that congregate yearly in a dazzling spectacle in the high mountains. It is the home of the Tarascan Indians, most of whom live around the highland lakes in the center of the state. Jalisco is more arid than its neighbor, and most of the land is used for ranching. It and its capital, Guadalajara, are the original home of many things Mexican, including *charros* (Mexican cowboys), the Jarabe Tapatío (Mexican hat dance), mariachi music, and tequila. Guadalajara offers what may well be the best shopping in Mexico in its suburb of Tlaquepaque.

Morelia

Morelia, the capital of Michoacán, lies 300 km (188 miles) west of Mexico City, about halfway to Guadalajara. It was founded by Spaniards under the first viceroy of Mexico and was meant to be a Spanish city. Its original name was Valladolid, after the city in

Castile; the name was changed after Independence to honor José María Morelos, who was born here and died for the cause. Most of the center of town, including the cathedral, is built in the lovely brownish-pink stone for which the city is known. City layout was planned in such a way as to set off the cathedral and principal churches to make the city appear more monumental.

☞ Morelia's **cathedral**, like most of the cathedrals in Mexico, is a mixture of different architectural styles; the beauty lies in how well these styles are integrated. In the case of this cathedral, it is done to perfection. The setting is ideal: it is flanked on both sides by plazas and in front by a broad avenue (Avenida Madero); this allows views of the cathedral from a number of perspectives. Except for the sheer size of the building, nothing is meant to be showy. The façade is a model of dignified restraint that harmonizes a predominantly classical style with baroque and mannerist flourishes. The towers are beautifully proportioned to accentuate their height. The cathedral is

Monarchs on the Wing

Every year, from November to February, a pageant of nature is held in a remote fir forest in the high mountains in eastern Michoacán. Monarch butterflies, the final link in a migratory chain that extends as far north as Canada, congregate by the millions. The flutter of their wings turns the fir trees into an enchanted forest. February is the peak of the season, and it's far better if the weather is sunny. There are several day tours from Morelia; ask at any of the main hotels. These trips make for a long day. If you have a car you might want to make the trip in a leisurely fashion by overnighting in the lovely village of Angangueo and perhaps taking the waters at the thermal baths nearby. Take the old Highway 15 to Mexico; you'll see the turnoff to your left before the town of Zitcuaro. The Sanctuary is open 8am–5pm. There is an entrance fee.

best viewed in the late afternoon sunlight, which sets the reddish stone aglow. Inside you'll find a magnificent organ, said to be the largest in the western hemisphere; in May, the cathedral is the setting for the annual International Organ Festival.

In the immediate vicinity of the cathedral are a few blocks of buildings with stone arcade fronts, called *portales* in Spanish. Under the portales along the main street are cafés that in the evenings become popular places for conversation and socializing.

On the same side of Avineda Madero as the sidewalk cafés, and in front of the cathedral, is the **Palacio de Gobierno**, a broad two-story colonial building that was originally a seminary. Note the great simplicity of its exterior, typical of the architectural aesthetic of most of the city. Inside are murals by Alfredo Zalce portraying the progress of Mexican history. Moving along Madero in the opposite direction, one block away, the visitor finds the former church and convent of the Jesuits. The church is now a beautiful public library. To the right of the library entrance is the tourist information office. The main entrance to the former convent, known as the **Palacio Clavijero**, is farther down this same side street. It is famous for its beautiful interior courtyard. Continue down the same street to a small plaza, across from which is the Conservatorio Las Rosas, the first music school founded in the Americas. The school is best known for its boys' choir, the Niños Cantores de Morelia. Inside you can find out if there will be any concerts scheduled during your stay.

On the street running behind the cathedral, cater-corner from the Plaza de Armas, is the **Museo Regional de Michoacán**, which covers the state's history in art from early Pre-Columbian clay figurines to colonial period religious paintings. A block farther down that side street, in front of the Baroque **Iglesia San Agustín**, are some portales that the city built to house food stalls in the evenings, where cooks wave morsels from their grills to tempt customers. Another evening sight is the illuminated Aqueduct of 253 arches that runs for

1½ km (1 mile) right into town. The Tarascan fountain at the end of the aqueduct also becomes illuminated.

Three blocks east of the cathedral is the church and convent of **San Francisco**. The large plaza in front has been overrun by street vendors in the same way as the portales have, while the former convent has been restored and is one of the most beautiful buildings in town. With its heavy buttressing and the cloister of small arches with Moorish elements, it looks more medieval than Renaissance. It is now the **Casa de las Artesanías del Estado**. Here you'll find the top line of Michoacán's enchanting handicrafts. The first floor houses a museum and store with beautiful displays of handcrafts of all kinds. On the second floor are small shops, each one representing one of Michoacán's craft villages. The museum and shops will give you a good idea of what to look for and how much to pay when you visit these villages and you might even see the artists at work. The center is open 10am–8pm, closed on Monday.

Pátzcuaro

An hour's ride from Morelia in the direction of Guadalajara is the sweet, peaceful, and picturesque town of Pátzcuaro, next to the highland lake of the same name. Pátzcuaro offers a sharp contrast in architectural style from Morelia. Here, the roofs are of tile, and the walls are of adobe covered in stucco and painted white (and, in the Indian tradition, have the lower portion painted in dark red). The rooflines, the walls, the sidewalks – everything is slightly crooked, giving the town a lived-in, unassuming feel about it.

This town was founded by the first bishop of Michoacán, don Vasco de Quiroga, as the episcopal see of the diocese and as the state capital. He chose this place next to the lake because it was the heartland of the Tarascan Indians (properly called the Purépecha). To this day the Bishop remains fondly remembered by the Indians of the area, who use the sobriquet "Tata" (grandfather) when referring to him. Tata Vasco was already an elderly man when he arrived in Mexico. He was a learned follower of the ideas of Erasmus and Thomas More, who hoped to establish in this area a cooperative society of villages, each dedicated to a specific craft such as weaving, pottery, wood carving, and lacquer-work, that would benefit the entire region. To this day, his division of crafts among the many lakeside villages remains intact, only now most of the production is geared toward tourists rather than neighboring villages. To get an idea of the different crafts to be found, visit the **Museo Regional de Artes Populares** and strike up a conversation with any of the museum attendants, who are from the area and have an intimate knowledge of the villages, then go to the **Casa de los Once Patios**

Long Live the Day of the Dead

Chocolate skulls, sugar skeletons, coffin cookies, bone-shaped bread. These are racked up by the millions for sale on the first and second of November, when all Mexico observes the Día de los Muertos, or Day of the Dead. Far from being mournful, the holiday is a celebration, a time for visiting cemeteries and having picnics by the graves of departed relatives. Food, tequila, cigarettes, and sweets are prepared as annual offerings for the departed and are placed beside family altars in the home on 1 November, All Saint's Day. Later, or on the following day, All Soul's Day, the dishes may be eaten at home or taken to the graveside and consumed in a party atmosphere.

The native religions of Mexico regarded life and death as two sides of the same coin, as a continuum, equally acceptable parts of human experience. After the Conquest, Spanish fatalism and characteristic preoccupation with death, rooted as much in the deep Islamic influence in Spain as in medieval Catholicism, fitted neatly with the Indian temperament.

The Purépecha Indian celebration attracts many tourists to Lake Pátzcuaro. Many communities that ring the lakeshore hold vigils in the cemetery all night to commune and honor their dead. If you wish to attend, you must make hotel reservations months in advance.

Mexico dreaming...The sun god makes an appearance at Lago de Pátzcuaro.

(House of the Eleven Patios), which now houses many handcraft shops. Also, don't forget to visit the market, which is located in the Plaza Chica and surrounding streets.

The Purépecha Indians, who you will see everywhere when traveling through the region, are linguistically unrelated to any other Indian group in Mexico. The closest language to theirs is one spoken by natives of Ecuador. Anthropologists are unable to account for such a migration, but this seems to be the case. In pre-Columbian times they were mainly farmers and fishermen, and they defended their territory successfully against the Aztecs.

Lago de Pátzcuaro, among the highest lakes in the world at 2,200 m (7,250 ft), dominates the region. Green volcanic mountains ring the lake, and promontories burst from the surface to form three islands. Janitzio island rises steeply to a monumental statue of

Morelos, raising a clenched fist skyward. Morelos is always portrayed with the scarf he wrapped around his forehead to ease his chronic migraines. Boats run out to the island every 20 minutes or so from the dock on the outskirts of Pátzcuaro town.

All around the lake are villages in which virtually every house is a workshop. Santa Clara del Cobre is known for its copper; Quiroga for inlaid gold lacquerware; Tocuaro for its masks; San Jerónimo Purenchécuaro for embroidery; Jarácuaro for straw hats; San José de Gracia for its dark green pottery; and Ocumicho for grotesque animal figurines. The best Mexican guitars are made in Paracho. The town of Pátzcuaro produces woven fabrics; the Tarascan capital, Tzintzuntzan (pronounced sin-SOON-san and meaning "Place of the Hummingbird"), makes pottery.

From Pátzcuaro a scenic mountain drive of about an hour brings you down to the avocado orchards of **Uruapan**. The town is also famous for its hand-painted lacquerware. Uruapan is the ideal base for visiting the now-dormant baby volcano **Paricutín**. One day in 1943, a cornfield began to bubble and smoke; when it stopped nine years later, a 600 m (2,000 ft) cone covered the cornfield and a number of surrounding villages. You can see the tower of a church poking through the black lava field. Horses can be rented at Angahuan to visit the moonscape scene. Uruapan's lacquerware has floral designs on boxes and trays – perhaps inspired by the tranquil floral landscape now protected as Parque Nacional Eduardo Ruiz National, extending from the city limits to the Rio Cupatitzio and its waterfalls.

Guadalajara

From Morelia, Pátzcuaro, or Uruapan, the quickest way to get to Guadalajara is to drive north to the super toll highway 15D. Both this road and the old Highway 15 pass by Lago Chapala. The lake is Mexico's largest, 83 km (52 miles) long. Bordering the shores of this lake are a few towns with large populations of Americans and Canadians, such as Chapala, Ajijic (ah-hee-HEEK), and Jocotepec (ho-ko-te-

103

PEK), artsy-craftsy communities that the expatriates have made their own.

An hour beyond the lake is Guadalajara, which Tapatíos (the nickname for Guadalajarans) call the "The City of Roses." It's a modern metropolis spread over a gently sloping plain at a comfortable 1,550 m (5,000 ft). With 5.5 million people, it is Mexico's second biggest city. To get at Guadalajara's special treasures, save time and energy by taking the inexpensive taxis and horse-drawn calandrias.

A good starting point is the colonial district around the **cathedral**. Begun in 1558 when northwestern Mexico was called Nueva Galicia, this imposing church is a blend of many styles, including rather "un-Mexican" gothic spires erected after an earthquake in 1848. The gothic interior of the cathedral is its most impressive feature, and the painting of the Virgin above the sacristy door is said to be by the Spanish painter Murillo. Four spacious plazas that open the heart of the city for strolling flank the cathedral. On the south side is the town's main square, the **Plaza de Armas**, with an elaborate Art Nouveau bandstand made of wrought iron. Facing it is the 18th-century Palacio de Gobierno, a beautiful building inside and out. The central staircase provides a

Blowing off steam; an erupting geyser acts up at Ixtlan, Guadalajara.

dramatic setting for José Clemente Orozco's masterpiece picturing an overwhelming Father Hidalgo avenging the sufferings of the poor with purificatory fire. The side panels, in Orozco's violent imagery, lampoon religion and depict the horrors of war.

On the opposite side of the cathedral from the Palacio de Gobierno is the **Museo Regional de Guadalajara**. The museum houses a large collection containing everything from fossils to archeological artifacts, colonial painting to contemporary ethnography. Note the section on *charros*, the fancy-dress gentlemen cowboys – an extravagant charro costume is worn by mariachis. Jalisco is the epicenter of both these Mexican traditions. Behind the cathedral is the Teatro Degollado, built in the 1870s and recognizable by its Classic façade with statues of the muses adorning its portico. The interior of this theater is beautiful. Check for concert schedules. Performances of the folkloric ballet (said to be one of the best in Mexico) take place every Sunday at noon.

Behind the theater, a long, open-air mall called the Plaza Tapatía leads to the **Hospicio Cabañas**. This former orphanage houses a cultural center. Its chapel walls are completely covered by powerful black and gray Orozco murals expressing the artist's pain at man's cruelty to man. On the cupola overhead is his famous mural *Man of Fire*. (More of his best work, done between 1935 and 1939, is in the auditorium of the university on Avenida Juárez.) Around the corner from the Hospicio, the huge two-story **Mercado Libertad** is the city's boisterous central market. Leather goods are a specialty here, particularly the huarache sandals of woven leather thongs.

But if you're serious about shopping, you can have no more pleasant experience than strolling door-to-door down the pedestrians-only Independencia of the nearby suburb of **San Pedro Tlaquepaque** (20 minutes from downtown by taxi). On this and other nearby streets are found the most sophisticated shops in Mexico, offering everything relating to arts, handcrafts, furniture, and jewelry. Pottery is what Tlaquepaque was traditionally known for, and it remains the most popular craft in the town. If you're interested in pottery, don't miss the Museo Regional de Cerámica and the Museo Pantaleón Panduro, showing masterworks of the potter's art. At the center of the suburb (once a separate village) is **El Parián**, where at night you can enjoy great mariachi bands. Another village swallowed by the city, Tonalá, a bit farther east, is a very popular shopping place, especially for pottery, blown glass, and wrought iron.

A very popular side trip from Guadalajara is a visit to one or more of the tequila distilleries in the nearby town of **Tequila**. The drive takes only an hour, but the most fun way of visiting the town is to take the Saturday train called the Tequila Express, which is operated by Guadalajara's Chamber of Commerce. Tequila tasting starts almost as soon as the train rolls out of the station.

THE PACIFIC COAST FROM MAZATLÁN TO ACAPULCO

Starting with the casual, sport-fishing port of Mazatlán, you can follow the coast south past charming Puerto Vallarta and down the exclusive Costa Alegre beyond Manzanillo, through laid-back Zihuatanejo to the dazzle of Acapulco. You're bound to find a place in the sun that's just right for you, and along the way travel through some spectacular tropical scenery.

Mazatlán

Mazatlán has long been famed for sport fishing and as the shrimp capital of the universe. Long-established clubs and modern hotels dot the beaches, and golf courses, a modern marina, and extensive tennis facilities add to the town's naturally inspired attractions. Despite the diversity of ways to enjoy time here, Mazatlán has yet to catch the attention of enough tourists to drive prices to the levels of other Pacific-coast resorts. This is good news for travelers looking for economy in a beach resort, for Mazatlán offers one of the top vacation values in Mexico.

Although Mazatlán may not have reached preeminence as a resort, it is a city in its own right, with the largest port between Los Angeles and the Panama Canal, and a population of nearly 500,000. There are elegant reminders of its history in the old downtown district – among them, the lovely **Teatro Ángela Peralta**, a national historic monument built between 1869 and 1874. Other sites of interest include the small but attractive **Museo Arqueológico de Mazatlán**, and the **Acuario Mazatlán**, a wonderful aquarium with adjoining botanical gardens.

Puerto Vallarta

Puerto Vallarta's appeal sneaks up on you – maybe it's the glimpse of a burro loaded down with palm branches clopping alongside a taxi; maybe it's the sight of laughing children being photographed by their family on one of the waterfront public sculptures; the glimpse of brilliant bougainvillea spilling over a balcony up a side street; or, perhaps it's seeing one after another perfect sunsets meeting the expanse of blue bay from the vantage point of a *malecón* bar.

White on white: stylish and slightly surreal, the Hotel Las Hadas beach, at the perennially popular Puerto Vallarta.

No matter what it is that draws you in, no other place in Mexico so perfectly combines the gentle feeling of a traditional *pueblo* with the convenience and comforts of a sophisticated resort.

For those who choose, there is refined dining, plentiful taxis, and an impressive collection of galleries showing an equally impressive representation of Latin American art. Or there are remote beaches with *palapa* restaurants whose owners personally bring in the catch of the day, challenging hikes to spectacular mountain waterfalls, and diving to the tonal songs of seasonally migrating humpback whales. There are also organized city tours, animated booze cruises around the bay, and a growing array of clubs with live music that ranges from mariachi to reggae.

Puerto Vallarta, or Vallarta, as regulars call it, is the most popular Pacific Coast resort. It is still small enough to charm, while having grown gently into its current size. It neatly divides itself into five key areas – knowing the particulars of each area helps you select a place to stay that best fits your preferences. Here's a rundown, from north to south: **Nuevo Vallarta** is actually located in a different state to the north, Nayarit, and has evolved into a sister destination of Puerto Vallarta. Ultra-modern hotels – many of them all-inclusive – front the wide stretch of beach here, giving a secluded sense of privacy. It is also the place to kayak in a lagoon or swim with dolphins. **Marina Vallarta** is modern and sophisticated – a resort within a resort – with a championship golf course and exclusive marina filled with yachts, sailing vessels, and charter boats. This fashionable neighborhood is a favorite with families, and offers top quality hotels plus abundant watersports, tennis, shopping, restaurants, and nightlife. Along the **Hotel Zone**, wide, soft beaches front an ample mix of excellent hotels and offer a great place for recreational watersports. **Viejo Vallarta** is the signature cobblestone village extending to the north and south of the Cuale River. It is Mexico at its traditional best. From family-run beachfront hotels in the "Zona Romántica" to eclectic inns poised on the surrounding hills, here is where you feel the essence of Vallarta's charms, and is preferred by independent travelers and repeat visitors.

Extending from Conchas Chinas along the **South Shore**, the landscape changes to dramatic mountains that tumble toward the sea. Tucked into the private coves of this coast is where you'll find a collection of full-service hotels made to order for honeymoons and romantic escapes. At the end of this stretch of shore, you'll come to Mismaloya Bay, where you can still climb up the ridge to the ruins of the set built for the film *Night of the Iguana*. Ava Gardner played opposite Richard Burton in John Huston's film, but it was the romance between Burton and Elizabeth Taylor that got the headlines and started the Hollywood Vallarta vogue. The white houses and cobbled streets of downtown Vallarta are populated with restaurants, bars, boutiques, jewelry shops, and art galleries. Buses and trucks roar through the center on Highway 200 with a deafening clatter. A refreshing, shady retreat is Isla Río Cuale, an island found between bridges on the river. Birds twitter, men read the papers over a cup of coffee, and a little girl plays with an iguana outside a shop that sells the same reptiles – though stuffed. Adjoining the upper bridge, the town market has a range of handicrafts on sale.

Cruise ships and sport-fishing boats dock at the marina north of town. From the marina, sailboats cruise across the bay to **Yelapa**, **Las Ánimas**, and **Quimixto**, a trio of isolated coves on the jungle edge and accessible only by sea.

The northern shore of Banderas Bay, about a 30-minute drive from Puerto Vallarta, is lined with relatively undeveloped beaches, including Destiladeras, La Manzanilla, and El Anclote. Also to the north, a new, luxury resort development is underway, anchored by the Four Seasons, and its adjacent Jack Nicklaus-designed golf course.

Traditional Mexican farming life goes its unhurried way just a little way out of Puerto Vallarta, up steep mountain roads to the east. **San Sebastián**, a 17th-century mining town, remains locked in time in its seclusion high in the Sierra Madre mountains. Accessible by excursion bus or a brief flight, a day in this picturesque town offers travelers a glimpse at life in another century, and another state of mind. The simple and the sensational seem to coexist easily here.

Costa Alegre to Barra de Navidad

Traveling south along the coast between Puerto Vallarta and Manzanillo you'll pass through a stretch of extraordinary beaches. The 240-km (145-mile) coast road, connecting tropical forests with dramatic cliff-lined coves, follows what is known as the Costa Alegre, or "Happy Coast." It's mostly an area of exclusive, privileged resorts, but also offers some simpler beachfront places to stay. You come here for privacy, seclusion, and immersion in nature, not for glitter and organized activities.

The loveliest section is the **Costa Careyes**, 120 km (75 miles) north of Manzanillo. The few hotels and lavish villas scattered on the hillsides above a chain of little coves enjoy privacy and unparalleled views. The road rises and falls, twists and turns as it crosses ridge after jungle ridge, sloping steeply westward like the backs of great green animals leaning down to drink from the sea. **Barra de Navidad**, a 16th-century Spanish base for Asian exploration, and San Patricio-Melaque are at opposite ends of a 5 km (3-mile) beach backed by a lagoon. Both little towns have a languid atmosphere and inexpensive accommodations. A favorite way to spend the day is to walk the beach one way, savor some seafood at an outdoor restaurant, and take a shuttle bus back.

Manzanillo

Manzanillo, at the southern end of the Costa Alegre, has been around a long time. The harbor beneath the knob of the **Cerro de la Cruz** (Hill of the Cross) was used for shipbuilding and the Pacific trade in the 16th century. The string of beaches to the north, where mountains come down to the sea, have long welcomed a steady winter clientele who enjoy small, comfortable hotels and the chance to explore the countryside. But it was the construction of a dream-resort complex, **Las Hadas** ("the Fairies"), by the Bolivian tin multimillionaire Antinor Patiño that put Manzanillo on the jet-set map, especially after it was featured in the movie *"10."* Las Hadas has spawned construction up and down the adjoining beaches; there are golf clubs, condominiums, and villas, and a strip of hotels, bars, and restaurants.

The town of Manzanillo is undistinguished, except for delicious fresh shrimp and fish brought in from the working port. A sailfish tournament is held in November and charter boats go out for other big game fish all year round. It also has a small but excellent archeology museum, the **Museo Universitario de Arqueología**, which exhibits a collection of pre-hispanic artifacts. Shops seem overloaded with novelty T-shirts and curios made from shells, such as a truly curious Christ crucified on three clams. **Las Brisas** beach, closest to town, is broad and uncrowded. It leads to **Playa Azul**, **Las Hadas**, **Playa Santiago**, and a succession of sheltered coves. Pelicans and frigate birds, soaring champions of the Pacific, are endlessly fascinating as they patrol the shore.

Ixtapa-Zihuatanejo

When Puerto Vallarta began to become a household word, the avant-garde of beachcombing discovered **Zihuatanejo** (pronounced *see-wah-ta-NAY-ho*), a fishing village between Manzanillo and Acapulco. It had what they wanted: a sparkling bay divided into intimate beaches by outcroppings of rock and wooded knolls, the simple pleasures of swimming and sunning, and the freshest of fruit and seafood, not to mention cheap beer and rum.

The secret didn't last long. FONATUR, the government agency that created Cancún, picked the area for its next venture, **Ixtapa** (*ees-TAH-pa*). Now the pair, only 9½ km (6 miles) apart but separated by the mountainous terrain, make an admirable parlay: Zihuatanejo for the charm of a village and its necklace of beaches, Ixtapa for manicured luxury on its own long beach, two good golf courses, tennis, windsurfing, and all the amenities of a top resort without the traffic and hustle of an Acapulco. Its hotels are ultra-modern, designed to fit harmoniously into the tropical environment. Minibuses shuttle back and forth between the two towns, or you can rent a moped for independence.

Zihuatanejo has grown more sophisticated, with boutiques and candle-lit restaurants overlooking the bay, but fishermen still bring in their catch at the town dock. From here, you can take a boat out to the rocky point at **Las Gatas –** ideal for snorkeling and diving.

While Zihuatanejo is better known for its beaches and its fishing-village ambiance, it has one of the better archeological museums on Mexico's Pacific coast. The **Museo Arqueológico de la Costa Grande** traces the history of this area from pre-Hispanic times – when the place was known as Cihuatlán – through the colonial era. Most of the exhibits prove that the area was an important trading zone for centuries, with items from far-off cultures such as the Teotihuacan and Toltec. Also of interest is a visit to la **Barra de Potosí**, 45 km (27 miles) south of Zihuatanejo, an idyllic fishing village surrounded by coconut and mango plantations, with a clutch of simple restaurants right on the beach. The social center of Zihuatanejo is not a zócalo, as is the rule in most Mexican towns, but a basketball court. La Cancha is the gathering place where bands play on Sunday evenings and vendors offer tamales and *elotes* (corn), along with sweet, home-made popsicles flavored with chocolate, cinnamon, and vanilla.

Acapulco

For years, Acapulco was principally responsible for Mexico's attraction to international travelers. Acapulco's fame was launched as the kind of place for which the phrase "jet set" was invented, the winter playground of the pampered. The publicity that follows the glamorous resulted in the city's growing popularity as a tourist resort, and it currently attracts upwards of 3 million guests a year, the vast majority from within Mexico.

Lifestyles of the rich and famous... Acapulco's glitzy appeal almost singlehandedly placed Mexico on the tourist map.

The first view of Acapulco coming in from the airport is of a sweeping bay, with white ships on blue water, a long curving beach lined with high-rise hotels, and the city cradled in the arm of green hills. It looks like a large, rather unkempt city, almost incongruous as a beach resort. However, after the sun sets and the lights begin to sparkle, you understand why Acapulco still holds such an allure to travelers – the view of the bay at night is especially stunning. Acapulco's great bay was discovered in 1523 by one of Cortés's lieutenants sailing in a ship carried in pieces by Indians across the Tehuantepec isthmus. Later, galleons sailed to Acapulco from Manila, bringing porcelain, silks, and ivory. To defend this treasure against pirates, the **Fuerte de San Diego** was built in 1617. Today the fort is a museum that traces the early history of the city. The fort is between the yacht harbor and the zócalo. It is open daily except Mondays 11am–5pm.

There are some 20 beaches in the Acapulco area. The main strip in front of the big hotels facing the bay is about 11 km (7 miles) long and quite broad, with room for the many sunbathers and siesta-takers. Few people swim along this stretch of beach, due to its reputed lack of cleanliness. If you do, be aware that there is a strong undertow at times: watch for the notice of swimming conditions posted at hotels.

Once the big beach was considered to be a series of beaches, still identified by bus stop signs along the six-lane main drag, **La Costera Miguel Alemán**. Now they have more or less merged into one. La Condesa is in the center of the bay and at the heart of the hotel zone action. To its left is Playa Icacos and the navy base with its three-masted training ship; to the right are Morro, Hornitos, and Hornos beaches and the harbor for yachts and deep-sea fishing boats. Hornos has restaurants and changing rooms and is backed by a public park. Beyond, the walkway of the Península de las Playas closes the bay. Its beaches, Caleta, Caletilla, and Angosta, are in coves with no surf. Launches from Caleta run regularly the short distance to La Roqueta island, where the swimming and diving is good from several beaches connected by paths through the woods. Older, smaller hotels and clusters of aging villas mark this peninsula as the original center of Acapulco tourism in the 1930s. Farther on are the cliffs of **La Quebrada**, world renowned for the divers who plunge from its heights into a narrow inlet.

From La Quebrada it's a short walk downhill to Acapulco's non-touristy zócalo area. The square is so overhung with trees that it's cool even at midday. It's backed by an Art Deco cathedral that began life as a cinema. Cafés flank two sides. You can buy a paper, have a coffee, and people-watch people who aren't just more people-watchers. For a moment you might forget this is swinging Acapulco, but at night you'll be aware that a busy red-light district is nearby. Behind the zócalo, along Avenida Cuauhtémoc, is the working world of shops and dentists and bus stations for the million citizens who aren't on holiday.

The big hotels have pools with swim-up bars (which were invented here), tennis courts, water skiing, and parasailing off the beach, and more or less continuous entertainment – from beach and pool sports to Mexican music and dance festivals. At most there will be plenty of shopping on the premises, and a choice of in-house restaurants serving Mexican or international cuisine. In town there are plenty of comfortable hotels with none of these extras, but very reasonable prices. They are found on the inland side of the Costera Miguel Alemán; just walk across the boulevard to swim.

Off the beach, Acapulco offers a lot to do. You can hop in a horse-drawn, balloon-draped calandria and clip-clop along to the Playa Condesa area's boutiques and the bars that have "Happy Hour Now!" displayed at all hours. From the harbor, depart for any one of the numerous sunset cruises, swimming and dancing cruises, open bar "booze cruises," or glass-bottomed boat cruises. You can pass the afternoon on one of four golf courses, at a bullfight (on Sundays only), in the jai-alai arena, or tearing down a the Rio Papagayo in a jet boat. For children there's the **Parque Papagayo**, with amusement rides, open at 4pm; and at the Centro Internacional de Convivencia Infantil (CICI), with a wave pool (with a giant slide) and a dolphin show.

For surfers, whale watchers, and other naturalists, a Baja sunrise marks the beginning of a tranquil day.

For next to nothing you can board one of the fuming, roaring buses and ride south along the coast, beyond the naval station, and over the ridge to Puerto Marqués. Here steep hillsides enclose a small bay and a beach solidly packed with open-air restaurants favored by the locals. It could be a million miles from the sophisticated luxury just over the rise. To the north, a half hour past La Quebrada your bus or cab will reach Playa Pie de la Cuesta, where the mangrove-lined Laguna de Coyuca on the other side of the highway was the location for parts of the *Rambo* movies. Bird-watchers might enjoy a "jungle cruise" on the launches waiting here.

It's after sundown that life begins for many in Acapulco, known for its nightlife as much as for anything else – nightclubs, discos, Mexican folklore, fiestas, and stage shows (for some reason, cross-dressing acts are a favorite). Many of the night spots and restaurants are up on the hills, where you can feast on the harbor view along with the lobster. Along the Costera, fish taco stands and ice-cream shops are open all night long, along with a new offering of beachfront bars – a more casual alternative to the glitzy hillside discos.

BAJA AND THE NORTHWEST

Separated from mainland Mexico by the Sea of Cortés, Baja (Ba-ha) is not quite Mexico. It is a curious mix of cultures, where the farthest point south, Cabo San Lucas, feels like a mere extension of the Southern Californian mindset just across its northern border. It is also a land of supreme contrasts and contradictions: most obvious are the emerald green golf courses appearing in desert landscapes and the luxury resorts rising in a land once known as a refuge for pirates and outlaws.

Baja defeated Cortés. He landed here in 1535 and later tried to implant a settlement, but this wasn't accomplished until a Franciscan mission was founded at Loreto in 1697. This was the first of a chain that was established nearly a century later up the coast in Alta California – as the present US state was called under Mexican rule. Baja began its tourist life as a fisherman's secret, a place where

Hollywood stars like John Wayne came in their private planes or yachts for fabulous catches of marlin and sailfish. Today, the secret is out – Baja is booming, with the fastest-rising popularity in Mexico. The 1,160-km (726-mile) Highway 1 skirts the peninsula's arid mountainous spine to connect Tijuana in the north to the southern tip at Cabo San Lucas, linking the few important towns and crossing the Tropic of Cancer on the way. Airlines fly in from Canadian and US cities. Resort hotels and condos are in place on gorgeous beaches and more are being built. With all these facilities, however, Baja is still peaceful and unhurried, with a rugged sense of itself, and the beaches are empty – in many ways this is still a paradise for travelers with a spirit of adventure.

Baja South

 Los Cabos ("the Capes") is the collective name for three places: Cabo San Lucas, the original fishing port at the Baja's southern tip; San José del Cabo, a traditional town; and the "Corridor," a spectacular 32-km (20-mile) stretch of coast that runs between the two. This area is the principle lure of Baja, and how most people come to know this outpost extension of Mexico. Flying in, you'll see this is cactus country – more than 100 varieties are found here, from tiny buttons to saguaros 15 m (50 ft) tall, and the weird, looping boojum, found only on the peninsula.

San José del Cabo is a conventional town, increasingly gentrified to feel like a blossoming artist's colony. The hotel zone is set apart from the town right on the beach, offering plenty of privacy. The blissful quiet is broken only by the pounding of the surf and the cries of sea birds. San José's golf course is a green oasis in the desert, with angular peaks of brown mountains rising some 1,800 m (6,000 ft) as a backdrop. Lack of humidity in the air sharply etches every detail miles away, and this dryness keeps you comfortable even when temperatures climb.

At **Cabo San Lucas** you'll be besieged by boat captains who want to take you fishing. There are at least a hundred kinds of craft for rent, from around 800 pesos per person for four sharing a power cruiser to half that price for a *panga,* a motorized skiff, including equipment and fishing license. The deep-sea fishermen come back around lunchtime. Rare is the boat that doesn't fly at least one marlin pennant, and there's almost always a big fish being hung up on the dock to be weighed and photographed with its captor. To conserve the species, no boat is allowed to bring in more than two. Others caught must be released, though after putting up a fight for an hour and being gaffed, many of these do not survive for long.

They call these fishing grounds "Marlin Alley," but there are an incredible 857 species of fish in the area. You'll see scores of

Big Grays of Baja

For whale-watching, Baja California is unsurpassed. Every winter in December and January, some 15,000 California Gray whales arrive along the coast at the end of a 8,300-km (5,000-mile) migration from the north. The females come to give birth and teach their calves how to come up for air in the warm, shallow waters of Baja lagoons. The Greys are up to 18 m (60 ft) long and the calves are 4 1/2 m (15 ft) long at birth. By March, after fattening on 190 liters (50 gallons) of milk a day, the calves are ready to make the long trip back north.

The main calving grounds are at Laguna Ojo de Liebre, also known as Scammon's Lagoon, about halfway up the peninsula, not an easy place to get to. Scammon was an American whaler who started the slaughter of the Grays that reduced their number to about 300 at the turn of the century. Now protected, they have made a strong comeback. You can see whales spouting and sounding in the open sea from Los Cabos. Or, you can take a whale-watch boat tour from the marina. Boats sometimes come so close that you'll get a splashing from the flukes of diving whales.

varieties on the ten-minute glass-bottom boat ride from the marina that takes you out to Los Arcos, where the blue Pacific slams into spray against pillars of granite as it mingles with the turquoise of the Sea of Cortés. Here, from a sand strip under eroded cliffs called Lover's Beach, you can snorkel in 30°C (86°F) water around the rocks where sea lions doze and pelicans perch. Climb up a bit and scan the sea: A whirl of white water marks big fish chasing little ones; a marlin jumping seems to stand on his tail.

Scuba divers come to San Lucas to witness the phenomenon of the **Cascadas de Arena**, an underwater sand-fall carried by currents to a point where it pours in a stream over the edge of a trench 270 m (900 ft) deep. Diving gear and lessons are available at the marina, and the pangas or well-equipped dive boats can take you out to diving and fishing sites. With luck, from December to March you might glide into a pod of whales.

Despite the wealth of natural attractions, it is the manmade golf courses that prove the prime draw to travelers here today. Six championship courses and one municipal course are open for play, with more planned, integrated into the new boom of luxury resorts. These high-priced accommodations, plus the fact that there's little agriculture in Baja and most foodstuffs must be shipped in, have resulted in higher-than-average prices in the Los Cabos area. Especially pricey are taxis – you should consider renting a car, even if only for a day, if you are at all interested in exploring.

La Paz, on the Sea of Cortés, is served by international airlines and is a short hop from Los Cabos. Or you can make the trip on a four-hour bus ride through starkly barren mountains where buzzards ride the thermals above deep canyons. La Paz was once famed for its pearl fishing, described in John Steinbeck's novel *The Pearl*. But the oysters died out fifty years ago and La Paz slumbered in the sun until the current Baja boom brought tourism. Some of the best diving and snorkeling is off the secluded beaches of Espíritu Santo island, a picnic day's sail from Pichilingue harbor, where the ferries from the mainland dock.

Giant cacti stand watch over the desolate landscape of rugged Baja North.

La Paz claims to have the most sensational sunsets in the world – the sea turns shades of red, and streaks of cloud ignite into flames as the sun disappears behind the dark purple bar across the bay. Patches of bright blue sky set off the livid clouds. The skyscape keeps changing until your film runs out, and then it gets even better.

Baja North

Tijuana used to be called "Sin City," but many a sin has been legalized since the bad old days of US Prohibition, and "TJ" today shapes up more as "Sale City," if tourist statistics are a measure. Tijuana is the foreign city most visited by Americans, and most come to shop. They say that more traffic passes under the Freedom Arch at the California border than at any other crossing in the world: some 40 million trips a year. It's

Take the Chihuahua al Pacífico rail through Copper Canyon, and you will be privy to scenes of unparalleled natural splendor.

so easy – not even a Tourist Card is required if you're staying less than four days and not going farther than Ensenada. Most of Baja California is a duty-free zone, so there are bargains on liquor and imported luxuries, plus incredible trash that somebody must buy or it wouldn't be here. The full range of Mexico's colorful crafts is on sale here, too, in the government's Centro Artesanal and in shops along Avenida Revolución or in the modern shopping mall in the Río Tijuana section. It has the pace of a perpetual clearance sale, pretty frantic at times.

Not as frantic as in the 1920s perhaps, when the Hollywood crowd and half the US Navy from San Pedro-San Diego used to line up at "the longest bar in the world." But there are still superlatives: the margaritas come in pitchers, the food at countless restaurants is authentically Mexican, and the nightclubs are as raunchy as you can get. There's plenty of sporting life out at the Hipódromo Agua

Caliente where *galgos* (greyhounds) race nightly at 7.45pm, and Saturday and Sunday at 2pm. Bullfights are scheduled every Sunday May–September in two rings.

The face of the new, commercial Tijuana, the fourth-largest city in Mexico, is presented by the fast-growing factories where low-cost Mexican labor assembles electronic products, and by the lively cultural center on the river, where there's always a fiesta of Mexican music and dance. But you don't have to look far to find the old face of Sin City still leering underneath the cosmetic clean-up.

The tollway south, Highway 1, quickly brings you to more sedate **Ensenada**, the long-established resort and fishing town on Todos Santos Bay, also Baja's busiest port. The drive down the cliff-lined coast is exhilarating, and you can stop to look for migrating whales, which navigate along the shore in December and January. In summer, watch the surfers. East of Tijuana is a rich agricultural area and the state's capital, Mexicali, and its California counterpart, Caléxico. The border crossing here leads to San Felipe at the top of the Sea of Cortés. Tides here drop 10 m (30 ft), compared to 1 m (3 ft) at Los Cabos. It's a weekend hangout for dune-buggy stunt drivers.

Copper Canyon

Copper Canyon is one face of Mexico most visitors never see, but those who do never forget it. The "canyon" is actually a vast network of canyons cutting deeply into the Sierra Tarahumara. This is a section of the Sierra Madre that lies between the coast of the Sea of Cortés and the high tableland of north central Mexico. Much of the fun is getting here, thanks to the *Chihuahua al Pacífico* railroad, which connects Chihuahua City to the coastal city of Los Mochis in the state of Sinaloa. It is nothing short of a spectacular ride – one of the great train rides of the world. The single-track line climbs 2,456 m (8,000 ft) to the rim of Copper Canyon. Along the way, the train passes through 86 tunnels and over 39 bridges, an engineering feat begun in 1898 by an American entrepreneur as part of his quixotic dream of linking Kansas City to the Pacific Ocean. Sixty-three years and $100 million later it was completed by the Mexican government.

It's best to go from Los Mochis so that you see the most amazing scenery (between El Fuerte and Bahuichivo) in full daylight. The first-class train makes the 672-km (420-mile) trip in about 14 hours, which includes a 15-minute stop at **Divisadero** on the rim of the canyon, allowing passengers to look down into the junction of three gorges more than 1,200 m (4,000 ft) deep. But to see more of the canyon area requires an overnight stay in **Divisadero/Barrancas** or in one of the other two principal stops in the canyon area: **Creel** and **Bahuichivo/Cerocahui**. At any of these towns you can find guides to take you hiking or horseback riding into the canyons or along the rim, or make a side-trip by car to one of the old silver-mining towns to be found at the bottom of the canyons. If you're going to stay at one of these towns, you should make reservations, because hotel rooms are few in number. October to early November and March are the busiest times of the year here.

> Mexicans prefer to orient people following the lay of the land. If the street has the slightest incline to it, you will probably hear some form of the verbs *subir* (to go up) and *bajar* (to go down), instead of right and left.

At any of the stops you make in the area, you'll find yourself in wild and beautiful canyon land with stunning mountain vistas, sheer rock walls, and strangely shaped rock formations. There's a tremendous variety of flora and fauna, too. Up at the top, in the rim country, pine forests predominate, while in the canyons the climate is subtropical, with many species of tropical trees, bushes, cacti, and wildlife. The region has several waterfalls, including **Basaseachic**, the tallest single cascade in North America.

This is also the land of the **Tarahumara** Indians. Totaling 50,000, they live in small settlements scattered about the region. These Indians practice elaborate rules of courtesy among themselves, which leads observers to call them shy. Those Tarahumara who deal regularly with tourists, however, have learned the ways of the outside world. Some Tarahumara women have little stands at Divisadero where they sell handcrafts, including pine needle baskets, wood carvings, and native-style musical instruments, but you'll see the Tarahumara at any of the towns in these mountains. They come and go as they please, without thinking anything of crossing on foot a canyon or two just to pay a visit to a friend. Their running skills and powers of endurance are legendary – it is said that they can outrun a deer.

Chihuahua

Chihuahua is a busy city of 1.5 million people, a five-hour drive south of El Paso, Texas. It was **Pancho Villa's** headquarters, and the house where his widow lived until 1981 is now the **Museo de la Revolución**. The best way to see this museum is with a local guide who will know all the stories about the fascinating life of Pancho Villa and his 23 wives, and can provide some context to what you see here. Included in the collection is the 1922 open Dodge sedan in which Villa was ambushed, and photos of him and his favorite troops sporting bandoliers and looking like bad *hombres*. Villa's grave is in Chihuahua, but it is empty. When he was reburied in the Revolution Monument in Mexico City, his body was found without a head – no one knows why.

The **Museo Quinta Gameros** is housed in a stunning mansion that provides the setting for a large collection of Mexican Art Nouveau furniture, which was brought from Mexico City. If you're a history buff, you may want to visit **Hidalgo's dungeon**, where the "Father of Mexican Independence" was held prisoner until he was executed nearby, at a spot where the **Palacio de Gobierno** now stands (also worth a visit for the building's architecture and murals).

YUCATÁN

The Yucatán is different from the rest of Mexico. Where all is mountainous elsewhere, the Yucatán is flat as a tortilla, a piece of the ocean floor pushed upward between the Gulf of Mexico and the

Caribbean Sea millions of years ago. This limestone slab is porous, quickly absorbing rainfall. Water percolates into the porous limestone, forming underground caverns and rivers. When the roofs of these caverns collapse, the water is exposed and the well-like formations called *cenotes*. The many cenotes in the area were very important to the Maya and, more than two thousand years ago became focal points for their communities, of which there were hundreds. Uxmal and Chichén Itzá have been the most extensively excavated.

In colonial times, this region far away from the viceroy's capital in Mexico City had its own governor. When Mexico gained independence, the Yucatán became an independent country and remained that way for two years. Then it decided to join Mexico, but in the political chaos of the following years, opted for independence again in 1846. The landowners, fearing an invasion force, armed their Mayan peasants, who promptly turned their weapons on their oppressors. The peasants' struggle to wipe out the European population from the peninsula is known in history as the Caste War; the Maya were almost successful. They were later defeated, but managed to keep de facto control of the remote eastern part of the peninsula well into this century.

In the 1870s, the fortunes of the peninsula rose again with the *henequen* boom. Henequen is a form of fiber harvested from a species of agave plant. It was used to make cordage and was in great demand up until the invention of synthetic fibers. Henequen production grew dramatically up to 1910 and the advent of the Mexican Revolution, from which the industry never fully recovered. It wasn't until the 1970s that the Yucatán found another boom. This time fortunes came in the form of tourism, and it began with the development of Cancún, which is now the most popular resort in Mexico.

☛ Mérida

Mérida, in the heart of the Yucatán, has been the most important city on the peninsula ever since its founding in 1541. It is a charming city of tropical, pastel-colored colonial buildings and grand 19th-century mansions, and you can tour it in charming fashion, too, by open bus or horse-drawn carriage. There is a lively street scene here in the evenings, when the city's inhabitants stroll about visiting with friends. Small shaded plazas with outdoor cafés provide popular places for people to congregate, and the main square never lacks for strollers. Besides strolling about, there is always something cooking in this town. Every night there is some dance performance or concert; most of these are free. To find out what's available, ask at your hotel or one of the tourism offices. Every Sunday, the city closes off a section off streets and plazas to hold a weekly fair called *Domingo en Mérida*, with concerts, comedy performances, food stalls, a flea market, and a book market, among other things. Later in the evening, a band plays mambos and rumbas in front of city hall, and people come to dance in the street.

Other pleasures include restaurants, museums, some interesting night clubs, and the best shopping in all the Yucatán. Items to shop for include locally made *hamacas* (hammocks), *guayaberas* (the traditional loose-fitting shirt worn in tropical Spanish-speaking countries in place of a suit), Panama-style hats made of finely woven fibers of the *jipi* palm, and the traditional dress, called *huipils* (heavily embroidered white cotton tunics worn by native Yucatecan women). The place to get Panama-style hats or *huipils* is in the handcrafts market, a couple of blocks

The colonial-style Plaza Principal in lively, picture-perfect Mérida.

southeast of the main square. The best places to find hammocks or *guayaberas* are the several stores that specialize in either of these items.

The old heart of Mérida is the main square, known by the locals simply as *el centro*. On the east side is the oldest **cathedral** in Mexico, which recently celebrated its 400th anniversary. It is an impressive structure devoid of elaborate decoration, and most of its stucco has fallen off, exposing the bare rock of the walls. This makes it look every bit of its 400 years. If the cathedral reminds you of a fortress, the resemblance is not without reason – it was built in the days of sporadic revolts by the region's Maya Indians. The interior is even more bare due to its having been sacked in 1915 during the Mexican Revolution. The former bishop's palace, beside the cathedral, now houses Mérida's **art museum**. On the south side of the plaza is the **Palacio Montejo**,

Hammocks

Hammocks are for residents of the Yucatán what beds are for us. Yucatecans will sleep in them all night long and complain when they are forced to sleep in a bed. Because Yucatecan net hammocks do such a good job of distributing weight, they are more comfortable than the knotted rope hammocks and the canvas hammocks commonly seen in the United States. But how do you measure the quality of a net hammock? Width would be a good way, but for the fact that these hammocks can be stretched as wide as you want. Weight is a better measure. A hammock that weighs about 1½ kilos (about 3½ pounds) is thought to be of good quality. If you get a lighter hammock, by the time you have stretched it out wide enough to lie across it diagonally (which is how you are supposed to sleep in them), the threads are so far apart that you can feel them against your skin. The knitted part of the hammock should be of fine cotton string and be at least 2 m (6 ft) long. The general rule is that the finer and the more numerous the strings, the more expensive the hammock.

where the Montejos, the conquistadors of the region, lived. It is a lovely building with Plateresque ornamentation, now occupied by a bank. Descendants of the Montejos lived in the house until the 1970s. Across from the plaza from the cathedral is the **Ayuntamiento** (city hall). On the second floor are the council chambers and a balcony with a view of the square. On the remaining side of the square is the **Palacio de Gobierno** (Governor's Palace). Go inside and you will see some extravagant murals by a local artist of fame, Fernando Castro Pacheco.

During Mérida's heyday, from 1880 to 1910, millionaire henequen planters built their mansions on the **Paseo Montejo**, Mérida's own Champs Élysées. Today, most of the boulevard is occupied by banks, airline offices, and fashionable restaurants. Of the old mansions that remain standing, one of the finest is the **Palacio Cantón Rosado**, now housing a wonderful anthropology museum that can help you make sense of what you see when you go out to the ruins. Look for the explanation of Mayan numbers, a bar and dot system, and the exhibit showing how the heads of infants were deformed by binding them between two boards to produce sloping foreheads. To meet Mayan beauty standards, teeth were filed and eyes made cross-eyed by dangling a bead before them. The museum, on Paseo Montejo where it crosses Calle 43, is open every day except Monday.

From Mérida, you have a choice of many side trips. There are several old henequen haciendas that have been restored into museum-restaurants or hotels. These are lovely places, perfect for those looking for a peaceful getaway. Less than an hour east of town is **Izamal**, a quiet town where horse-and-buggy is the most common form of taxi and the attractions include a large 16th-century monastery and the remains of a pyramid and other ruins that were never completely torn down by the Spaniards. Just northwest of Mérida is **Dzibichaltún**, the ruins of a small Mayan city, with a small museum on site. Beyond the ruins but still not far from Mérida is the port of **Progreso**, where Meridianos like to go to the beach. Due west of Mérida is the offbeat fishing town of **Celestún**, from where you can hire a boat to visit the flamingo colony in the **Celestún Wildlife Refuge**. In addition to the flamingos, many other bird species thrive here. South of Mérida, an hour and a half away, is the famous Maya city of Uxmal, and nearby, the other ruins that are part of the Puuc Route.

Uxmal

The road to **Uxmal**, pronounced *Oosh-mal,* 82 km (50 miles) south of Mérida, goes straight through Yucatán's low scrub thickets and past some fields of agave. En route, at **Yaxcopoil** you can visit a 17th-century hacienda museum to see how the planters lived and the way henequen fiber is extracted from the agave. The curious little sacks hanging in trees along the way are black oriole nests.

The Uxmal ruins are the finest examples of a Mayan style called **Puuc** (pronounced *pook*), named after the low Puuc hills of this district. It is characterized by rectangular buildings, square columns, and an upper frieze panel decorated

Uxmal: Governor's Palace (inset) and view across the ruins (right).

with intricate projecting geometrical mosaics. Many panels are covered with masks of the rain god **Chaac**, an ugly fellow with a curling trunk snout and swirly eyes. You'll notice these upper sections are slightly angled outward. The Mayans never mastered the true arch, but came close with the pointed **corbel arch** of overlapping stones. Lintels over some doorways are made of the original sapodilla wood, one carbon-14 dated at A.D. 569. The wood is so heavy it doesn't float in water.

Straight ahead as you enter the ruins is the **Pirámide del Adivino** (Pyramid of the Magician). The path from the entrance passes a *chultún,* or cistern, to collect rain, the only source of water in this area, which has no cenotes. Consequently, the rain god was the all-important deity. Approach the steep three-tiered pyramid with rounded corners from the rear and climb 120 steps to the top. (There is a safety chain you can hang onto for the climb; just don't look back.) The

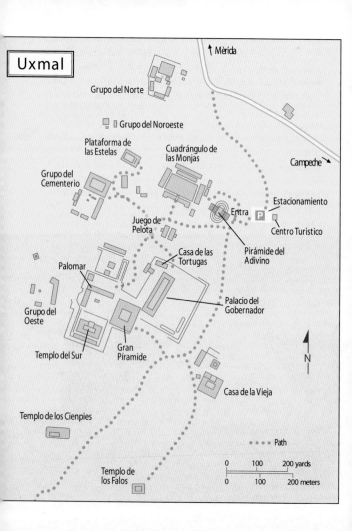

pyramid was built in stages between A.D. 600 and 900, each stage covering the preceding one. Moving around to the front side, you'll get a good look at many Chaac masks on the corners of the temple doorway. The door itself is the mouth of a giant mask. From this vantage point you'll see the other principal ruins spread out beneath you and many other still unexcavated mounds in the thick brush beyond.

Directly in front is the **Cuadrángulo de las Monjas** (Nunnery) – incidentally, names given to Mayan ruins are usually pure conjecture, and no one really knows the purpose of many of their structures. The grassy quadrangle is enclosed by four stately low buildings on different levels. On the east, the upper panel of latticework mosaic is decorated with inverted pyramids formed by double-headed serpent bars. The west-side frieze has a stylized snake weaving through it from right to left, with his head between the sixth and seventh doorways.

The more you examine Mayan buildings, the more the tangle of design takes on recognizable shapes. There's a feather canopy crowning a throne above the central door, where the face of an old man with a turtle body can be seen. Niches in the façade represent palm-thatched houses. This theme is repeated over the doorways on the south building, where 16 rooms may have been a kind of inn for priests on pilgrimages to Uxmal. Head south through a corbel arch, and follow a path through the **Juego de Pelota** (Ball Court) to the **Palomar** (Dovecote), so called because of the pierced triangular elements of its roofcomb. It is just one wall of a large, unreconstructed complex to the south. Rubble on three unrestored sides of the **Gran Pirámide** (Great Pyramid) suggests that the Mayans were covering it to build a larger one when Uxmal was abandoned around A.D. 1000. A small building, rather Grecian in its elegance and harmonious proportions, stands between the pyramid and the ball court. The stone tortoises decorating its upper frieze have earned for it the name **Casa de las Tortugas** (House of the Turtles) and it carries the symbolism of fertility and rain.

Continue on to the field fronting the imposing **Palacio del Gobernador** (Governor's Palace). The entire area is a man-made

Fishing boats moored at the harbor in Ciudad del Carmen, Campeche State.

platform. From a distance you'll be able to see that among the thousands of stones making up the façade (all cut without metal tools and fitted without mortar), projecting Chaac heads form an undulating serpent. The fallen column in the plaza is thought to have been used in astronomical observations. There are other partially restored ruins beyond this platform. The Casa de la Vieja (House of the Old Woman) is supposed to be the temple of a sorceress who, with her dwarf grandson, the Magician, tricked the king of Uxmal and became rulers of the city. Nearby is a building with phallic drainpipes. Beyond the Dovecote a path leads to the Grupo del Cementerio, a cemetery complex where platforms have skull and crossbones reliefs.

Uxmal's grounds are open 8am–5pm. A 45-minute sound-and-light show in Spanish starts at 7pm (8pm during Daylight Savings Time). Headsets are available offering narrations in English. The dramatized history tells the story of how Uxmal declined because of successive failures of Chaac to deliver the rains and, finally, as the result of a war that shifted power to other cities. There are four hotels near the site, three with swimming pools. Within an hour's drive of Uxmal are three other extremely interesting Mayan cities, Kabah, Sayil, and Labná. Paved Mayan roads once connected these cities.

Campeche

About three hours southwest of Mérida off Route 180 is **Campeche**, a Gulf of Mexico port city and the capital of the state bearing the same name. Here, as everywhere along the gulf side of the peninsula, the water isn't as clear and blue as it is on the Caribbean side; as a result, few tourists come here, and those who do are usually on their way from Mérida to Palenque or to the Río Bec region. Even so, the city is well worth a visit, a beautiful example of a lowland colonial town. In the 17th century, Campechanos constructed a high wall around their city with four gates and several bastions as fortifications against marauding pirates, who had already captured and sacked the city on two occasions. They also built **forts** (complete with moat and drawbridge) on each of the two hills above the town. Now, most of the wall is gone, except for two sections bordering the seaward and landward gates, which are quite impressive. On Friday and Saturday nights, there's an entertaining **sound-and-light show**, illustrating the history of Campeche, at the landward gate. The bastions and the forts are now museums housing models of sailing ships, an exhibition on pirates, Mayan votive stones from nearby sites, a botanical garden, and the contents of some tombs excavated from the ruins of Calakmul.

But most impressive is the city itself. Campechanos have renovated the entire old part of the city, restoring it as closely as possible to its colonial appearance. Simply strolling about the place is delightful; another way to see the town is by **trolley tour**, which leaves from the main square almost every hour. The best shopping is at a store run by the *DIF* (a social welfare agency) called **Tukulna** at 333 Calle 10.

Scaling old heights: the perfectly-preserved majesty of El Castillo, Chichén Itzá, lures many an energetic admirer to its summit.

The main attractions outside the city are the ruins of **Edzná**, less than an hour away in the direction of Mérida. The ruins of the **Río Bec route** are farther away and are perfect for the more adventurous traveler, since they are relatively recent excavations and much of the vegetation has been left as it was found. Federal highway 186, which goes through the Río Bec region, eventually crosses the peninsula to the southern Caribbean coast at Chetumal. Of the ruins along this route, the most impressive are those of **Calakmul** (classic Maya architecture in the heart of the jungle near the Guatamala border, tallest pyramid in the Yucatán), **Balamkú** (perfectly preserved sculpted walls showing Mayan kings and underworld deities), and **Becán**, surrounded by a dry moat. A trip through the region would take two days and require spending the night at one of the hotels around Chicanná or Xpujil. Several companies offer tours of the region from Campeche.

Chichén Itzá

Chichén Itzá, 120 km (75 miles) southeast of Mérida, is the best-preserved and biggest of the Mayan cities. It may have been settled around A.D. 500 by Mayans called "Itzá" moving north from Guatemala; in Mayan its name means "mouth of the well of the Itzá." The city appears to have been abandoned for the first time 125 years after its founding and re-occupied in about A.D. 900, after which its most important buildings were constructed. It was to be the last great achievement of Mayan builders. Chichén Itzá was abandoned for good after a war in 1182, though pilgrims continued to visit its sacred cenote for centuries. It is possible that Toltec warriors, perhaps led by the legendary Ce Acatl Topiltzín of Tula (Quetzalcóatl), captured Chichén Itzá around the year 1000. The ruins are in two sections, Chichén Viejo (Old Chichén) and Chichén Nuevo (New Chichén), roughly dating, respectively, before and after the Toltec conquest.

The Spaniards named the pyramid in Chichén Itzá's new section **El Castillo**. It is in fact a temple to Kukulcán (the serpent god) and evidently had importance in Mayan astronomy. There are four flights of stairs with 91 steps on each. Adding the top platform gives 365, the days of the year. The stairs divide nine terraces into 18 on each side, the number of months in the Mayan calendar. At 5pm on the spring and autumn equinoxes, a shadow moves down the right wall of the north staircase like the rippling body of a snake until it reaches the carved serpent head at the base; then it moves back up again – Kukulcán descending to earth and returning to the heavens! The phenomenon understandably attracts large crowds.

A hot, clammy, and crowded climb up a staircase archeologists built inside the pyramid in the 1930s takes you to the platform of an earlier temple that holds a red-painted jaguar with jade eyes and mother-of-pearl spots. This is no place for the claustrophobic. The north chamber of the temple atop the Castillo is decorated with carvings on columns and reliefs of priests in feathered headdresses. The

Plataforma de Venus, directly in front of the north staircase, is full of Toltec influence. The faces carved on the sides, with staring eyes and round ear plugs, are not Mayan. You'll find a carving of the Toltec morning star and its symbol, a graceful feathered serpent, around the top level, as well as a curious fish with legs (a tadpole, perhaps?). Traces of red and green paint are a reminder that this city, too, was once colored resplendently.

To the east stands the **Templo de los Guerreros** (Temple of the Warriors). The portico of square columns richly carved with warriors in armor fronts steep stairs to the top platform, where a Chac-Mool is centrally placed. These stylized figures are always the same – a reclining man holding a plate on his lap. They may have been stands for burning incense. The temple doorway is formed by snakes whose rattles bend overhead to hold the vanished lintel. More columns reminiscent of Tula form a portico on the south side of the temple called the **Mercado**, or market. No doubt these colonnades, when roofed, provided relief from the Yucatán sun. The south walls are covered with reliefs of eagles, bears, and jaguars. An earlier temple to the Chac-Mool underlies this complex.

A rough causeway some 275 m (905 ft) through the undergrowth leads from the Castillo to the **Cenote Sagrado**. It's a haunting spot, a well 59 m (194 ft) across, overhung with trees and vines. Here human sacrifices were thrown to propitiate the rain god in times of drought. The legend says the victims were beautiful virgins, but most of the more than 40 skeletons found by dredging were of children. A quantity of offerings in jade and gold have been recovered from the steep-sided well's murky green waters, some 22 m (65 ft) deep. Edward Thompson, the US vice-consul in Mérida, made the first attempt to plunder these riches. In 1903 he bought the entire site and an adjoining hacienda for $75. Some of his loot has been returned to the museum in Mérida; the rest is in US museums.

To the right of the main area is the **Tzompantli**, a wall of skull reliefs in black and white and decorated with eagles holding human

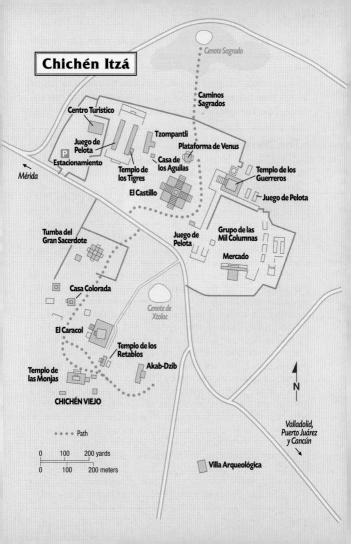

hearts in their talons, all very Toltec in spirit. Next comes the **Templo de los Tigres** (Temple of the Jaguars), built into the rear wall of the ball court. The reliefs on the lower-level columns describe the creation of the world. Legend has it that tears from the eyes of the god on the left pillar become waters that give life to plants and animals and then to man. The right pillar is a woman with a skull head representing

The Maya

Of the many Pre-Columbian peoples that have left behind ruins in Mexico, the Maya are the most fascinating. The puzzles of their origin and decline have obsessed generations of scholars. What we do know is that the Maya were settled in most of their homeland by 600 B.C. They were obviously influenced by the Olmec, to judge by some of the earliest artifacts that they have left us. A recently excavated façade in Chacán Bacán revealed Olmec-style masks. But these artifacts are rare enough to mean that the Maya weren't an Olmec people.

They seem to have borrowed extensively from the cultural achievements of the Olmec. It's not certain, however, whether their writing system or their calendar were such borrowings. If they did learn either of these things from the Olmec, they refined them greatly and developed wholly original features, which made uniquely Mayan. The 365-day calendar became extremely precise, allowing them to make equally precise astronomical predictions. Their mathematical system, multiplying by 20s, was the system used by the Olmec, but the invention of the zero was all their own. In the arts, the Maya seem to be all alone in the classic age. There is little similarity with any other culture before or after. But there seems to have been a great unity among the priest class of all the different Maya city states of the time.

What happened to this civilization? We have scant evidence and can only speculate. But in this the Maya share something with their contemporaries, Teotihuacán and the Zapotec, as well as several other cultures to come afterward.

Follow the trail to The Snail (El Caracol), also called the Observatory – one of Chichén Itzá's most unusual Mayan structures.

death. This duality of life and death is a constant theme of religious art in Pre-Columbian Mexico. In the center of the rear wall covered with warriors is a bearded figure who may be Kukulcán. The doorway of the upper temple is flanked by huge monolithic serpents. Inside are more warriors and fresco fragments of Toltecs fighting with Maya. The **Juego de Pelota** (Ball Court) is the largest in Mexico. The price of defeat, or victory, is vividly described in relief panels at mid-court: A headless captain with serpents streaming like blood from his neck kneels before his opponent, who holds the head and brandishes a knife. Note the protective pads, shoes, and costumes of the players.

Old Chichén Itzá is reached by a trail south of the Castillo. All along the way are the mounds of mostly unexcavated structures until you reach one of the city's most unusual buildings, **El Caracol** (The Snail), also called the **Observatory**. Situated in an open space, this round

Take the plunge: from ocean to pool, from aqua to turquoise, it's all variations on perfection in the Yucatán.

tower has an interior circular stair leading to the rooms where observations were made of Venus and other heavenly bodies. Farther on, the top-heavy one-room **Iglesia** (Church) and **Templo de las Monjas** (Nunnery) are temples heavily adorned in the Puuc style, with the curling Chaac snouts in evidence. The Nunnery was partly blown up by treasure hunters. The **Casa Colorada** (Red House), on a mound and with remains of a classic Mayan roof comb, is one of the oldest at this site, dating from the seventh century.

The southern section of the ruins is a 15-minute walk away, along a small path. Most of the buildings are semi-overgrown. On one, the

two atlantes holding up a door lintel are obvious copies of the warrior pillars at Tula. Other temples and houses are purely Mayan. Ruins in the brush are found in all directions, giving an idea of the vast extent of Chichén Itzá in its prime. A model and explanations in the visitor's center museum at the entrance are helpful in putting it all in perspective. All this is a lot to appreciate in one day; if you want to see the ruins thoroughly, plan to stay at one of the several comfortable hotels adjoining the site.

Near the ruins is the **Balankanche** cave, discovered in 1959 and found to have been used for Mayan rites. It takes a bit of squeezing and stooping to get through to the chambers where offerings to the rain god were made. Jars and an altar have been left as they were found beside a pool where blind fish swim. Tours of the cave can be in either Spanish or English, but require a minimum of six people. Farther east, some 40 km (25 miles) in the direction of Cancún, is a lovely cenote called **Dzitnup**. You can take a swim here in the clear water illuminated by a sunbeam shining through a hole in the ceiling.

Cancún and Isla Mujeres

Cancún is the point of introduction for the vast majority of travelers to Mexico. Aquiline waters, white sand, luxury hotels, a sporting nightlife, and even nearby archeological wonders all serve as lures to the more than two million visitors who come here each year.

Cancún may be soul-less (at least anyone looking for adventure and exotic environs will find it so), but this region offers the ideal combination of breathtaking natural beauty and the depth of Mexico's thousand-year-old history.

These magnificent Caribbean beaches were the first face of Mexico seen by Europeans, at least as early as 1517. For well over four centuries Quintana Roo, as the Caribbean coast of Yucatán is known, was left to the few rebellious Mayans who could scratch a living in the brush; for everyone else it was a remote place of exile. A small Mayan ruin, **El Rey**, speaks to the fact this was once Maya land – although obviously an outpost, not a true settlement.

By now the story is well known: the government's tourism developers, FONATUR, fed a "wish list" into a computer to locate the ideal place for a beach resort. The computer answered "Cancún." The uninhabited 22-km (14-mile), hook-shaped island had to be developed from scratch, but it had everything nature could provide: an average 243 sunny days a year, a fantastic beach on one side, and a tranquil lagoon on the other. As an added touch, Mayan ruins were not far distant. To construct and service the playground, a new town, Cancún City, was built on the mainland, and short causeways connected it to both ends of the island. Only super-deluxe hotels were permitted on Cancún (good cheaper ones have been built in town), and roads and an airport had to be installed. The luxurious complex opened in 1974, and Cancún's fame rapidly spread. Today it is undisputedly Mexico's top resort.

It's easy to get around in Cancún: buses and taxis travel between the row of towering hotels that front the beach like a line of dominoes along the length of its one street, Paseo Kukulcán. More than 20,000 rooms in the area offer something for every taste and budget. Most of the dining, shopping, and entertainment is found at the northern "hook" of the island, near the **convention center**.

Sporting vacationers take to the tennis courts or golf courses, and scuba diving and deep-sea fishing is popular from cruisers and catamarans. But shopping seems to be one of the most popular pastimes in Cancún, with its profusion of grand malls selling everything from designer sunglasses to duty-free jewelry and perfumes. There is a more traditional alternative among the handicraft stalls of the **Mercado de Artesanías** on Tulum Boulevard in Cancún City. For some authentic color, there's a bullring in town, with *corridas* year-round on Wednesday at 4pm. By night, a taste of true Mexico is imported for fiestas at the hotels and the folkloric dinner show at the Convention Center. Among the most popular night-time venues, however, are the many internationally recognizable clubs and bars. The **Forum by the Sea** houses an impressive collection of nightlife in one seaside entertainment mall.

If you are at all curious to see the real Mexico, leave the beach and glitter long enough to enjoy one of the many interesting day-

Pick a palm-thatched palapa and soak in the simple, pristine beauty of a Cozumel beach

excursions. Among the most popular day-trips are to the great Mayan city **Chichén Itzá** (see page 137), to the ruins of **Tulum** (see page 149), or down the coast to a string of marvelous beaches, some completely untouched, others with bungalows or palm-thatched palapa shelters for hammock-slinging, and a few with first-class hotels catering to scuba divers. **Punta Bete**, 60 km (37 miles) south of Cancún,

Underwater heaven: Second only to Australia's Great Barrier reef, Cozumel's reef is a diver's dream.

has good swimming off a picture-postcard beach with coco palms. **Akumal**, 104 km (65 miles) from Cancún, is famed for diving. There's even an underwater museum where you can swim among cannon and other artifacts found by divers. **Xcacel** (pronounced sha-SELL), 120 km (72 miles) south of Cancún, is another very attractive and uncrowded swimming beach. Xcaret, 72 km (50 miles) south of Cancún, and Xel-Ha, another 60 km (36 miles) farther down the coast, are both extensive ecological theme parks, with swimming, snorkeling, and other water-oriented activities, as well as restaurants, shops, changing rooms, and organized activities. Both are attractive, but you'll leave thinking how beautiful they must have been before the buses came.

Although only 10 km (6 miles) from Cancún, **Isla Mujeres** is quite another world. This "Island of Women" was named as such for the numerous Mayan fertility idols found by Cortés when he arrived here in 1519. Today it is favored by those who appreciate the convenience of flying into Cancún, but prefer a more easy-going, laid-back pace. The beaches are exquisite, the snorkeling and diving are excellent, and there is an ample selection of casual, beachfront restaurants. Accommodations range from budget-beach style rooms to super-luxury guesthouses, with the common denominator being travelers who have an appreciation for tranquility. Ferries from Puerto Juárez just north of Cancún or Punta Sam (cars carried) take passengers over to the island for an enjoyable day of exploring, or for longer stays. Swimmers head for **Playa del Norte**, snorkelers for **El Garrafón**'s coral reef. A curiosity for expert divers are the underwater caves where "sleeping" sharks lie on the bottom. The island is only 2 km (1½ miles) wide and 8 km (5 miles) long, with the concentration of hotels, shops, and seafood restaurants at the northern end.

Cozumel

The island of Cozumel, 20 km (12 miles) off the Yucatán and roughly 50 km long and 15 km wide (30 by 9 miles), lies near the northern end of a barrier reef of coral that is second only to Australia's Great

Barrier Reef. The coral reef produces white sand and prevents waves from roiling the bottom, and the result is crystal-clear, light aquamarine water of a temperature that is warm but not tepid. In other words, these waters are absolute heaven for swimmers, snorkelers, divers, and even passengers on a glass-bottomed boat.

A proficiency card is required for scuba diving, but instructors will deliver one after alarmingly few hours and will act as guides on reefs of varying complexity. Palancar Reef is 5 km (3 miles) long and drops sharply into a trough 1,620 m deep (5,350 ft) with 75 m (250 ft) visibility. San Francisco Reef, about 545 m (500 yds) long and 15 m (50 ft) deep is easier, and Yacab, 9 m (30 ft) deep is fine for beginners. Boats to the reefs and **Parque Chancanab** at hotel docks pick up passengers and provide refreshments and gear. The underwater population is gaudy: delicate blue angel fish, black-and-white striped sergeant majors, red squirrel fish with big eyes and a spiny back, intense, electric-colored schools of tiny wrasse dazzling like a cloud of sparks, butterfly fish with a round black spot, yellow and silvery grunts, and rainbow-hued parrot fish are just a few of the common varieties close to shore. Farther out you might see a ray flap by like a giant bird. The marine park at Chancanab is a good place to learn to identify the varieties and to get quite close enough to a moray eel.

With so much to see in a calm sea, fewer people swim in the hotel pools. Poolside is great for sunning, socializing, and snacking. Beachside, there's tennis, windsurfing, parasailing, chasing about on the noisy waverunners, and sailing, as well as cycling. Near midpoint amid the beaches along the western side of the island, iguanas scuttle in the modest Mayan ruins at **San Gervasio**. Turtles come ashore in July to lay eggs near Punta Molas.

San Miguel is basically a giant shopping mall interspersed with a few lively restaurants and bars, where margaritas are served in goblets the size of goldfish bowls. The din of rock music from radios is constant and heavy traffic gets noisy along the seafront Malecón. Hotels offer evening entertainment, but while there are discos in town, Cozumel isn't really big on nightlife. It's fun to join the crowd at outdoor tables around the zócalo and walk back to your hotel escorted by fireflies. In winter, cruise ships unload up to 2,000 passengers a day in an assault on the shops of San Miguel, where most Mexican handicrafts and some designer clothes are found. Shop owners put up permanent signs reading "Welcome passengers of the…" and hang up a new ship's name every day. Prices are quoted in dollars, which are practically the second coin of this realm. To get away from it all, as you may well be tempted to do, board one of the charter boats go out for game fish from the harbor.

A ferry connects with buses on the mainland at **Playa del Carmen**, a very popular beach spot for those who are interested less in snorkeling and diving and more in having a good beach vacation with lovely water, quirky surroundings, good restaurants, and fun nightlife. It's about 45 minutes away by ferry from Cozumel. The town also has a central location, perfect for getting to nearby ruins or to other spots up and down the coast.

> **A handy term for market-goers:** *¿Cuánto cuesta?* (How much is it?)

Tulum and the Lower Caribbean Coast

By Mayan standards **Tulum** was a small trading city, built around 1200 when Mayan architecture had become decadent. Surrounded by a wall with five gates, it most probably had to be defended during the wars that contributed to the decline of the Mayas in Yucatán. Tulum's glory is its setting. The **Castillo**, the central temple on a high platform, commands an incomparable view over the sea and coast. Perfect little beaches spread out below. The deity worshipped in Tulum was **Yumkin**, the "Descending god," always shown diving head first. It is thought he represented the setting sun. Central to Mayan religion was the fear that the setting sun might not return from his journey into the underworld. The **Templo de los Frescos** (Temple of the Frescoes), in the center of the compound, has faded paintings inside and out of offerings to the god, and of fish and fertility figures. A stucco relief of Yumkin holding a snake fills a niche by the door. Notice how the cornice angles form faces. Yumkin is seen again over the entrance to his own temple to the left of the Castillo.

Of special interest is a stretch of ancient road dividing the compound. Though they didn't have wheeled vehicles, the Mayans did build paved roads, called *sacbeob*, perhaps for ceremonial processions. More of these may be seen at **Cobá**, a very interesting eighth-century Mayan site on lakes some 40 km (25 miles) inland. A network of sacbeob crosses Cobá's mostly unexcavated ruins, which extend into the jungle. Cobá was evidently a very large city, probably founded by Mayans from Guatemala, for the very steep pyramids here are similar to the ones at Tikal. At Cobá you can share the archaeologist's feelings of discovery as you follow jungle trails surrounded by mysterious mounds. Bring insect repellent and wear walking shoes.

The beaches along this part of the coast are solitary and pristine. Just south of Tulum is the **Punta Allen peninsula**, which is a perfect place to get away from the crowded beaches to the north. At the very tip is the town of Punta Allen, a lobstering village. The peninsula shelters a lagoon that is part of a large biosphere reserve called **Sian Ka'an**; much of the coast here is mangrove, and inland it gives way to tropical forest and savanna, with abundant wildlife including jaguars, howler monkeys, manatees, and endangered turtles. Some visitation is permitted in the buffer zone of the reserve.

Farther south on highway 307 you see a turn-off for the **Majahual peninsula**, a favorite place for divers who come to explore the **Chinchorro reef**. If you get here, you will have left civilization pretty far behind you. Should you remain on 307, you come to **Laguna Bacalar**, a freshwater lake 100 km (60 miles) long that is as clear and blue as the Caribbean because it is fed by cenotes.

Finally you arrive at the end of the line, the state capital, **Chetumal**. This city has one good thing going for it: the wonderful **Museo de la Cultura Maya** (Museum of Mayan Culture) with all

Looming over solitary stretches of beach, the ruins of Tulum command an imposing and magical presence.

kinds of interactive exhibits that explain some of the Maya's cosmology, astronomy, calendrics, and society. It is a modern, beautifully laid out museum. From Chetumal you can go either to Belize or inland and follow the Río Bec Route (see page 136).

OAXACA AND CHIAPAS

Visits to this region of beautiful highlands, endless beaches, and impressive jungles are never long enough. The colonial jewels of Oaxaca and San Cristóbal, with their large Indian populations, are fascinating places for simply watching and listening. When the urge to do something more active strikes, there are many ruins, Indian villages, and solitary vistas to seek out. Or, perhaps you simply want to relax by the ocean and enjoy some Oaxacan beach culture.

Oaxaca

Oaxaca (pronounced wa-ha-ka) is the state that seems to have everything – beaches, highlands, handicrafts, and ruins. And now, with greater air access to the state's capital and beach resorts, there is less reason not to go. But if you fly directly in and out of the resorts without paying a visit to Oaxaca City, you will have missed one of the most charming colonial cities in Mexico.

Oaxaca City will slow down your clock. The pressure is off the minute you settle into a chair at one of the cafés bordering the central gathering place, the **zócalo**. There's plenty to do, but why rush? Enjoy a *café con leche* or a *cerveza*, and have your shoes shined while you watch the world go by. Streets around the plaza and the adjoining Alameda are open to pedestrians only. A balloon seller ambles past, kids playing tag will dart and squeal around the fountains, an Indian woman with her hair carefully

> Whether you're visiting a museum or looking for a place to eat, two terms to keep in mind are *abierto* (open) and *cerrado* (closed).

braided will hold up for your appraisal a belt she has woven, and the rich aroma of sizzling food from a sidewalk stall floats by. As afternoon turns into evening, the bandstand lights up, dimly, and the municipal band serenades the strollers who come just to wile away a little time in such lovely surroundings with marimba music or old-fashioned waltzes. Soon, it's time to head for a restaurant and enjoy some of the food for which Oaxaca is famous.

There are no big modern buildings in Oaxaca. Most of the downtown area was built in colonial times with the lovely green stone for which the city is famous. All buildings tend to be low and broad with thick walls – an architectural style that was born from several serious earthquakes that struck the city during the colonial era. Even the churches' bell towers are low and squat, as is the case of the **cathedral**, which has been reconstructed a couple of times. The façade presents the viewer with all the elements of the highly stylized Oaxacan baroque with its heavy and elaborate framing of the main panels, the wave-like depiction of clouds, and the detailed depiction of its principal scene, the assumption of the Virgin. The overall effect is one of solidity and stateliness.

The famous Mixtec gold mask and breastplate at the Oaxaca Museum.

Indeed, many of the loveliest buildings in Oaxaca are churches and convents. The most beautiful is **Santo Domingo**, set back on a plaza six blocks north of the zócalo. The church and convent were begun 1575 and rebuilt with walls 2 m (6 ft) thick after being destroyed by an earthquake. More destruction resulted from the Wars of La Reforma in the second half of the 19th century, when Santo Domingo and its monastery were used as a barracks and stable. In 1898, the church was beautifully restored under the guidance of Bishop Gillow. The barrel vault and walls are encrusted with ornamental gilt stucco and paintings, made more dazzling by a white plaster background and black outlining. St. Dominic stands in the center of the golden three-tiered main altar screen. The sumptuous **Capilla del Rosario** (Rosary Chapel) to the right attracts the most devotees. The ceiling just inside the entrance is covered by a many-branched genealogical tree, with mustachioed grandees and queenly dames representing the ancestry of St. Dominic. It culminates not in the saint, but in a Virgin and child, added during restoration. A magical moment may envelop the church when an Indian woman, kneeling in a shaft of light from the stained glass windows, spontaneously lifts her voice in a hymn.

The monastery next door stayed in hands of the government, which recently performed an impressive restoration to the entire building and surrounding grounds. It now houses an ambitious museum, the **Museo Regional de Oaxaca**, that presents in several galleries the story of the region from the arrival of the first inhabitants to the first large civilizations, to the conquering Spaniards, to the long colonial period, to Independence, to the Reform walls, all the way to the present. There is also an ethnology exhibit on the present Indian population of the surrounding valleys. A lot can be learned in a visit here that

will be helpful when visiting the villages and ruins that lie in the surrounding area. Clearly, the centerpiece of the museum's collection is the Mixtec treasures found in Tomb 7 in Monte Albán. More than 500 pieces of jewelry and artifacts were found in this tomb in 1932. Here is the famous gold burial mask and breastplate, a necklace of gold turtles, huge pearls, jewelry of coral, amber, and jade, cups of rock crystal, and a skull partly

A young girl learns the craft of weaving, for which her state – Oaxaca – is renowned.

covered in turquoise mosaic. Other skulls show traces of brain operations – but no indication whether the patients survived.

The Mixtecs mastered the art of crafting gold by the "lost wax" method. The form was first carved in clay, then covered with wax, and overlaid again by clay. The wax was melted and drained and the cavity filled with molten gold. Then the clay was removed and the

Markets in the Valley Villages

Each village in the valley of Oaxaca has its own market day, and each its special product. The Sunday market in Tlacolula is one of the best. On the way, stop at the Tule Tree, an ancient ahuehuete cypress, an incredible 60 m (164 ft) in circumference. A short detour to Teotitlán del Valle brings you to the valley's most famous weaving center. Along the road you'll see fields of maguey, the spiked leaf agave grown here to make mezcal, a local tequila. You can visit a distillery to see it done and to sample the product. Tlacolula merchants will show you how to drink it straight, with a special reddish salt that has powdered maguey worms in it. Some bottles come with a gusano (worm) inside to prove it's the real thing.

The Friday market in Ocotlán is not very touristy, and the Thursday market in Zaachila even less so, but they couldn't be more picturesque. The market women don't particularly like having cameras stuck in their faces, though – so be respectful and ask before you click. See the many varieties of fresh and dried chile peppers, watch how each fruit is polished and piled artistically, notice how the mangoes are carved like pine cones. You'll see women wearing the very shawls, blouses, and red-and-black skirts sold in Oaxaca's craft shops. (Alas, beware of pickpockets in the crowds.) San Bartolo Coyotepec, on the road to Ocotlán, is the source of velvety black pottery. Stop at any of the houses with pots outside to see them being made.

gold image polished to perfection. In another room you'll find some of the glass beads the conquistadors traded to the Indians for gold. If they had found Tomb 7, they would have melted the treasure into ingots, as they did with most Indian gold. The museum is open 10am–8pm, Tuesday–Sunday.

Another marvelous collection is in the **Museo Rufino Tamayo** on Calle Morelos. The painter, a native son who died in his 90s in 1991, converted a colonial house and patio and filled it with his superb selection of ancient Mexican art from every period and civilization. Look for the charming little Olmec "sunbathers" in room 1, the clay model of a ball game with spectators and a great helmeted Nayarit warrior in room 2, and in room 3, two amazing terracotta figures, an old man "chewing herbs" and an enthroned figure of the skeletal God of Death, among the many masterpieces. This museum is open 10am–2pm and 4–7pm, closed Tuesday.

The **Basílica de la Soledad** two blocks farther east honors the city's patron saint, whose image appeared miraculously at this spot in a box on the back of a mysterious burro. This Virgin is extremely popular throughout the state. There's a fun little museum behind the church to the left that exhibits in random order all kinds of memorabilia and honor paid to the Virgin. In the plaza in front you will find a several ice-cream vendors (it's a sort of tradition to eat ice-cream after visiting the basílica). Also for sale are religious curios, including little *milagros* – small tin images of legs, arms, hearts, or animals that the faithful buy to pin up in the chapel of their favorite saint as a form of petition.

Oaxaca has a large festival every July called the **Guelaguetza**, which showcases the costumes and dances of the many Indian villages in the state. It is a popular festival that fills the city for two weeks. On the last two Mondays of the month there are performances of the region's dances in the large outdoor amphitheater on the Cerro del Fortín hill. On preceding Sunday nights, university students dance the *Bani Stui Gulal* in the plaza in front of La Soledad; this is the history of the region presented through dance.

Mitla boasts 15th-century Mixtec palaces and courtyards in splendid condition.

The markets of Oaxaca and neighboring villages would be sufficient reason for your visit (see pages 198–199). Oaxaca is particularly famous for its **weavings** (especially those colored with cochineal and other natural dyes), **black pottery**, and **alebrijes**, which are wood carvings of fantastical animals. For other items, Indian *tianguis,* or street markets, are all over town and women and children offer their wares wherever you turn. Unusually fine handicraft shops occupy the interiors and patios of colonial mansions. Look for most of them on the pedestrians-only Alcalá and Cinco de Mayo, streets that run north from the plaza to Santo Domingo. But there's also daily action in the covered **Mercato Benito Juárez** behind the zócalo and on Saturday in the sprawling **Mercado de Abastos** west of the Periférico loop. Both are places where the populace comes for supplies. Each section has its own cloud of scents: sweet, fermented, spicy, floral, fishy, and so on. And each has stalls heaped with the freshest, most colorful produce. You'll find straw hats and baskets, embroidered blouses, rugs, shawls, and sandals in the covered market. The quality may not be as high as in the craft shops, but they're authentic; Oaxacans buy them too. Bargaining is part of every transaction. Early on Saturday, Indians from the countryside come into the **Mercato Abastos** with chickens and pigs, hand-made brooms, and sacks of charcoal. When they've done their business, they fill up with enchiladas wrapped in banana leaves at the numerous food counters. Another place to try, particularly if you're looking for apparel or weavings, is the **Mercato Artesanías** at the corner of J.P. García and Zaragoza.

Mitla

Trips to the markets can be combined with visits to some of Mexico's most interesting ruins and attractions. The road to Tlacolula continues on to **Yagul**, 35 km (21 miles) east of Oaxaca, and Mitla. Most tours sail right past Yagul, but the pleasure of exploring this city of Zapotec and Mixtec influence is well worth the short detour. From the crumbled fortress with its cactus sentinels, you look down on a roofless labyrinth of a palace, a ball court, and the full sweep of the valley. Perhaps because it has only been partly excavated and is usually empty of visitors, Yagul can seem to be your own discovery.

Mitla comes next, about 40 km (25 miles) east of Oaxaca. The ruins are right in the village. These palaces and courtyards of 15th-century Mixtec design were inhabited at the time of the Conquest and most were used, rather than destroyed, by the Spaniards, which explains their excellent state of preservation. The exception was the temple, as usual now covered by a church. The palaces are unlike anything you'll see elsewhere. They are covered by panels of projecting mosaic composed of little limestone bricks tightly fitted without cement. The concept is unique and the work that went into it immense. Because some of the designs resemble the scrollwork of Greek friezes, they are called *grecas*. The massive stone lintels and pillars were somehow dragged from a quarry 20 km (13 miles) away.

Across the road, the **church group** of three patios shows that the mosaics were originally painted white on a red background. Mitla is a Zapotec town today and the local guides will claim the palace-builders were of their ethnic group. Who can blame them? In the town, the **Museo Frissell**, open 9am–6pm, exhibits Zapotec figurines found in the valley by American archaeologists based here.

Monte Albán

Monte Albán, atop a high ridge 8 km (5 miles) west of Oaxaca, is an astonishing sacred Zapotec city that for more than 1,200 years embodied the grandeur of one of ancient Mexico's most important civilizations. The site itself, a mountain falling off steeply on all sides into valleys, is quite extraordinary. Around 500 B.C. the mountain crest was leveled by enormous effort to create a ceremonial plaza 300 m long and 200 m wide (980 by 650 ft) for temples, a *juego de pelota* (ball court), an observatory, and palaces for the priest-rulers. In A.D. 700 all this was abandoned, though the surrounding hillside was later used as a burial ground (where the Mixtec treasures of Tomb 7 and other finds have been unearthed). Apparently the ancient city was closed to all but priests and nobles. The remains of the houses and terraced fields of the peasantry who supported them covered the mountain, where many unexcavated mounds are visible.

Lifted into the open sky, Monte Albán seems designed as a meeting place of men and gods. One can easily imagine how dazzling the plaza must have been when its monumental structures were covered with plaster and painted red and white. The pyramidal platforms originally held temples and palaces of wood. If you're on a tour or engage a guide, you'll probably begin by circling the ruins from behind in order to visit **Tomb 104**. Burials were usually beneath the floors of houses. Descending steps into this one, a flashlight is

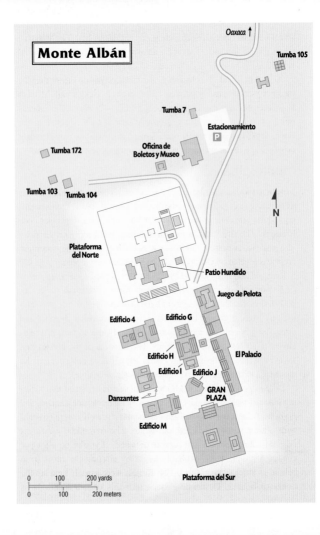

needed to see the head of a rain god and some faded frescoes over the entrance to the crypt. Then a path through the underbrush emerges on to the **north platform**, overlooking a sunken patio and the whole complex. To the right, a massive platform covers an earlier building. Again a flashlight is needed to enter a narrow passage and see the original carved façade inside.

The next structure shelters the **Danzantes**, slabs carved soon after 500 B.C. showing naked men and women in gesturing poses that earned them the name of "dancers." They have puzzled archaeologists for years. Some appear to be swimming, others are deformed, or are apparently cut open to expose their organs. Some have beards or negroid features alien to the Zapotecs, but similar to some Olmec faces. They may represent prisoners of war. One theory is that they are a kind of medical textbook, illustrating illnesses and surgical operations.

The arrow-shaped structure at this end of the plaza (Building J) is angled eastward and has a star symbol on its base, giving rise to the idea that it was aligned to serve as an observatory. Carvings of upside-down (i.e. defeated) men and hieroglyphic symbols on the walls, however, support the argument that it was a monument to military conquests. Monte Albán writing is different from the glyphs of the Olmecs and Mayas and has not been completely deciphered.

The view from the top of the partly excavated **south platform** is superb, taking in the three mountain ranges converging on Oaxaca. The eastern line of buildings is called **El Palacio**, for it may have been a palatial residence. In the center of the plaza are the remains of a temple and its staircase. Leaving the complex, on the right is a small **ball court**. The stone "seats" on one side seem too narrow for spectators. Were they part of the game? This is another of many Mexican mysteries proving that "nothing is more difficult to predict than the past."

There's a museum exhibiting carvings and models that help explain Monte Albán's successive phases and its relations with the contemporary cultures of Teotihuacán and the Mayas. Some 500 years after the city's unexplained abandonment, the Mixtec tribe moved

Margarita, anyone? This laid-back, no-frills beach restaurant exemplifies the tone of Puerto Escondido.

into the valley and ruled over the Zapotecs. They used Monte Albán as a cemetery, sometimes appropriating Zapotec graves. When the Aztecs dominated Mexico, the Mixtecs retreated to the hills, where they live today, while the Zapotecs stayed on in the valley. There are good crafts shops and a cafeteria in the museum. Monte Albán is open 9am–5pm. Mini-buses from Oaxaca run direct to Monte Albán from the Hotel Mesón del Angel at Calle Mina 518.

The Oaxacan Coast

The Pacific Coast that borders Oaxaca state has become known as the area to travel in Mexico, if what you are looking for is a pristine, wild, unspoiled stretch of beach. The first to gain recognition was **Puerto Escondido**, considered one of the world's top surf sites. Its renowned **Playa Zicatela** is nicknamed "the Mexican Pipeline," and is the site of an annual competition during the fall swells. Throughout the year, the town attracts a young and very hip international crowd, with its laid-back village ambiance, attractive and value-priced accommodations, and nearby nature excursions. At the center of town is a curving beach, where fishermen land their boats and sell their catch on the spot. One street back is the *Adoquín,* a pedestrian-only stretch of street named for the hexagonal-shaped, interlocking bricks used in its paving. Hotels, shops, restaurants, bars, travel agencies, and other services are all conveniently located here. Though small, the town enjoys an active and varied nightlife, with a strong live music scene during winter months. From dining to hotels, Puerto, as it is called locally, offers one of the best overall beach values in Mexico. You can fly in from Mexico City or Oaxaca, or drive or take a bus along the scenic Mexican 175 highway through the mountains from Oaxaca. It's only 250 km (155 miles), but takes a full day.

A few hours by boat or down the coast road from Puerto Escondido is the even more laid-back **Puerto Ángel**. This place truly is a "sleepy little fishing village." You'll eat lobster or fish on the beach under a thatched palapa shelter and snooze in a hammock strung between two palms. Turtles come ashore to lay their eggs in this area, and one of the country's top turtle preservation facilities lies between Puerto Escondido and Puerto Ángel, in the constant struggle to protect this endangered species against poachers.

A few spots, such as several of the inlets along **Bahías de Huatulco**, are officially slated for development by FONATUR, the government agency that created Cancún and Ixtapa. Located 40 km (25 miles) to the south of Puerto Ángel, it has 36 beaches on a spectacular coastline spread across nine bays. The fact that the area has been slow to catch on has resulted in a curious mix of ultra-modern infrastructure, few distractions, and unspoiled natural areas. Huatulco has what it takes to attract visitors – including golf, tennis, water sports, fishing, a few restaurants and night spots, luxury accommodations, and direct flights from selected US cities – but hasn't developed its own distinct personality yet. For now, Huatulco is ideal for those who want to enjoy the beauty of nature during the day, then retreat to well-appointed comfort of a luxury hotel by night.

 # Palenque

In 1840, the intrepid American explorer, John Lloyd Stephens, and his artist-companion Frederick Catherwood came down from the Guatemala Highlands into the Mexican state of Chiapas, drawn by rumors of a Maya city in ruins. Near the village of Santo Domingo they were led by Indians into the jungle, and soon, to their elation, they were surrounded by massive stones. "We spurred up a sharp ascent of fragments, so steep the mules could barely climb it…Through an opening in the trees we saw the front of a large building richly ornamented with stuccoed figures on the pilasters, curious and elegant, with trees growing close against it, their branches entering the doors; in style and effect it was unique, extraordinary, and mournfully beautiful… Standing in the doorway, we fired a feu-de-joie of four rounds each, using up the last charge of our firearms."

The ruins of Palenque ("tree-surrounded" in Spanish) are still mournfully beautiful, especially when emerging from eddies of mist in early morning. Though major buildings have now been cleared, the grassy clearly closely hemmed in by low hills and dense rainforest contains only a fraction of the 500-odd structures identified so far at this massive site. Walk a few steps along forest paths and you are back in the jungle that still engulfs most of the city. Stephens recognized what sets Palneque apart from such overpowering monumental sites as Chichén Itzá. At Palenque, the workmanship is far more artistic and harmonious, less designed to inspire awe and with a practical bent. There are niches with platforms for sleeping and a steam bath; a pagoda-style tower, with its large windows commanding a sweeping view of the plain and forest, may have been a watchtower and has no counterpart in Maya architecture.

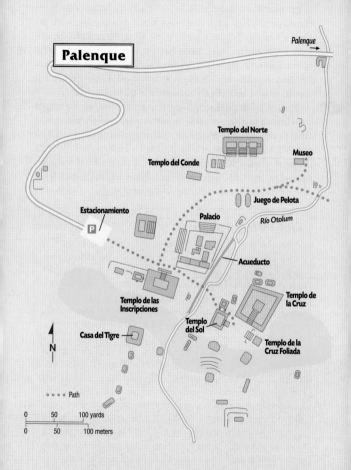

Palenque

Palenque →

Templo del Norte

Templo del Conde

Museo

Juego de Pelota

Estacionamiento

Palacio

Río Otolum

Acueducto

Templo de las Inscripciones

Templo del Sol

Templo de la Cruz

Templo de la Cruz Foliada

Casa del Tigre

N

····· Path

0   50   100 yards
0   50   100 meters

Palenque's prime spanned A.D. 500 to 900, the height of the Maya classic period. Nah-Chan (the Maya name, meaning "house of the serpent") was a city-state ruled by priest-kings, the greatest of whom were Pacal and his sons, Chan-Bahlum and Xan-Kul, who ruled from roughly A.D. 615–720. The last dated inscription in Palenque is 799, and sometime after that the city was invaded from the north. It appears to have been largely abandoned in the ninth century.

The **Templo de las Inscripciones** is an eight-tiered pyramid with 69 steps leading to a temple whose inscriptions are hieroglyphics, giving Pacal's pedigree. Chan-Bahlum is also represented on the pillars. This pyramid, handsome enough in itself, turned out to be unique – in 1952, the government archaeologist, Alberto Ruz l'Huillier, lifted one of the unusual paving stones of the temple and discovered a rubble-filled staircase. After four seasons of digging out stone and mortar to a depth of 21

Only Way To Go

Wherever there's a road in Mexico, there's a bus. The bus is the country's favorite mode of travel – very cheap, comfortable, and a good way to see the scenery and enjoy the people. First-class buses usually are first class, with air-conditioning and a bathroom; second class can be okay, but generally uncomfortably crowded. The two services usually operate from different stations. Head for the Central de Autobuses (or Camiones) de Primera Clase.

Directo doesn't always live up to its name. Especially on the outskirts of town, the bus driver will often stop to let people on or off. A lot of eating goes on during long bus rides. You may be offered a snack or a drink, and your neighbor will be pleased at your offer to share your own provisions. It's a good way to break the ice and strike up a conversation. Many drivers hang a motto over their seat. A favorite that may give you second thoughts: "If this is my last trip, God, may it lead to you." Not to worry – bus travel in Mexico is quite safe.

m (70 ft), Ruz came to a chamber where a stone box held some jade ornaments and a pearl. Battering through a wall 4 m (12 ft) thick, the workers found another room and in it a casket containing the skeletons of six young men, evidently sacrificed to guard a tomb. But where was the tomb? A huge triangular stone blocked one wall. Digging around it, Ruz broke into a third chamber and what he saw was "a huge magic grotto…delicate festoons of stalactites hung like tassels of a curtain, and the stalagmites on the floor looked like the drippings of a great candle… Across the walls marched stucco figures in low relief." In the center of the vaulted room, now opened for the first time in more than a thousand years, was a large slab carved with a jewel-draped figure wearing a feathered crown – the excited archaeologists brought jacks to lift the heavy slab. Another stone lid underneath was then removed. In a narrow sarcophagus lay the skeleton of Lord Pacal, his face covered

More Mayan mastery: Palenque's Temple of the Sun with its well-preserved roof comb and heavy stucco external friezes clearly visible.

The church and zócalo of San Juan Chamula, Chiapas. The church is filled with hundreds and hundreds of candles.

with a mask of jade mosaic. The body was surrounded by jade ornaments, and adorned with a collar, rings, and ear ornaments of jade. In a scene reminiscent of the opening of Tutankhamen's tomb in Egypt, Ruz had discovered the only known Maya pyramid built for a royal burial. The "ice" and "snow" were crystals from centuries of lime deposits.

The descent into this crypt down slippery steps is not all that pleasant on a crowded tour. At the bottom the carved slab lies in the center of a room 10 m (33 ft) long. A strange mortared duct leads from the tomb to the top of the stairs. It is believed to have been a way for Pacal's spirit to speak to the living world. The large, heavy slab had to have been placed here before the pyramid itself was finished, so the entire structure was likely built while Lord Pacal was still alive and made ready for his burial. The ornaments found in the tomb had been placed in the Museo

Nacional de Antropología in Mexico City but were stolen in 1985. The treasure was recovered and the museum's exhibit in a reconstruction of the tomb has now been reopened. A stone in the grass before the pyramid marks the grave of Alberto Ruz, facing the tomb he discovered.

A small stream that the Mayas paved over separates El Palacio from an amphitheater formed at the jungle's edge by the mounds of four beautiful seventh-century temples erected by Chan-Bahlum. The largest, on the left, is the **Templo de la Cruz** (Temple of the Cross), so called because of the cross-shaped tree of life design. To the right is a relief panel of a God of the Dead in a jaguar cloak, smoking a cigar; to the right Chan-Bahlum in leggings and a quetzal feather headdress. The crests of these temples are called "roof combs." The mansard slope of the roofs peculiar to Palenque copies thatch roofs still used today. The **Templo de la Cruz Foliada** (Temple of the Foliated Cross) straight ahead has key-hole arches and a panel with a leafy tree of life. The roof comb of the facing **Templo del Sol** (Temple of the Sun) is well preserved and so are the heavy stucco external friezes. Inside, Chan-Bahlum faces an underworld god against a heraldic device of shields and lances. The word in Maya for shield is Pacal, the dynasty's name. The small temple is called Templo XIV – here we find the ruler dancing before a kneeling female figure, presenting an offering.

Beyond the Palacio, the outlines of the ball court are visible; farther on are five temples called the **Grupo del Norte** (Northern Group), whose purpose is not known. To the left of this group is the **Templo del Conde**. A picaresque character named Baron Waldeck lived in its ruins in 1832. Waldeck was employed by the Irish Lord Kingsborough to help prove the theory that the Mayas were the Lost Tribes of Israel. Kingsborough refused to believe that such a civilization could have been created without influence from elsewhere. He rode his hobby horse into bankruptcy and died in debtors' prison.

A small **museum** in the trees past the Grupo del Norte must be visited, if only to see the superb terracotta portrait head of a Maya noble-priest. There is a fine panel of the coronation of Xan-Kul, who followed Chan-Bahlum. One of the figures holding his throne is mustachioed, and since Mayas, like most Indians, do not grow facial hair, the presence of bearded faces is always intriguing. Photographs show how the tomb of Lord Pacal looked when it was found. (The museum is open 9am–1pm and 2–5pm. The site opens at 8am and closes at 5pm.) Colectivos run to and from the ruins and town. Lacandón Indians sell bows and arrows under the trees by a refreshment stand.

There is a small airport at Palenque but the main airport serving the area is at Villahermosa on the Gulf coast, some two hours away by road. The town of Palenque has little of interest to the tourist, but there are hotels, a few with pools. For further excursions, a guide can lead you on horseback along trails to unexcavated ruins looming in the forest. Small planes from Palenque and Villahermosa can be chartered to visit the important Maya cities of Bonampak, with its famous frescoes, and Yaxchilán; both can also be visited on fairly arduous road safaris arranged through the hotels.

The bus from Palenque to San Cristóbal de las Casas takes nearly five hours to cover 207 km (128 miles) through the gorgeous foothills and Sierra Madre de Chiapas mountains of the southernmost Mexican state, Chiapas. This is real jungle, hacked away over much of the road's length by peasants growing maize on the steep hillsides by the ancient slash-and-burn method of land-clearing. One result is heavy soil erosion and landslides that wash out sections of the road every rainy summer. You'll remember there are no temples to rain gods in this moist region! Along the road, women sell bags of oranges and tacos. Some 58 km (36 miles) out of Palenque, the turnoff to **Agua Azul** (Blue Water) leads after 5 km (3 miles) to a nature reserve protecting a staircase of pools with water as blue as the sky. The river spills over projecting limestone platforms, each producing a low, foaming waterfall and a blue basin. The ledges and pools step down the hillside through green forest, an enchanting and unexpected refuge.

After Ocosingo, as the road climbs, you'll pass ragged coffee plantations where women and children rake beans to dry on the ground. The ferns, elephant-ear plants, and tall hardwood trees of the jungle give way to pine forests where wild lantana and dahlias brighten the hillsides. In these parts, nearly every male over the age of 12 seems to carry a machete and wear a straw hat. Mud and thatch huts look very much like the temples atop pyramids in Palenque.

San Cristóbal de las Casas

The charm of **San Cristóbal de las Casas** is its untouristy, strongly Indian flavor. Two Maya tribes predominate in the surrounding villages, the Tzotzils and the Tzeltals, with a few shy Lacandones turning up from the forest on market days. Each village has some identifying trademark in its costumes, but all the men wear knee-length white shorts. The Tzotzil-speaking men of Zinancantán wear hot pink tunics and flat hats trailing ribbons. The women wear blue wrap-around skirts and distinctive white huipiles embroidered with an ancient, intricate Mayan rectangular pattern in red. The men wear sandals, but most women go barefoot, and many carry babies in hammock-like *rebozos* slung over their backs. Their hands are always busy, weaving a colored belt or making a doll. When seated in the sun, they fold their rebozos like bath towels and place them on their heads.

The town is old Spanish, though without the flamboyance of the colonial cities of central Mexico, and its history is somber. The region was invaded in 1527 by a particularly cruel conquistador, Diego de Mazariegos, whom Cortés had sent on a punitive expedition because the local tribes were behind in their tribute payments. Mazariegos founded the town and called it La Villa Real de Chiapas. He captured Indians, branded them, and sold them as slaves. This brought him into conflict with **Bartolomé de las Casas**, a Dominican friar who had sailed with Columbus and had become a staunch protector of the Indians. Las Casas, whose name the town now bears, became bishop of Chiapas in 1545. (You saw him in Diego Rivera's mural in the Palacio

Nacional in Mexico City, shaking his cross at the conquistador.) The region had no wealth to attract settlers, and such administration as there was came from Guatemala. Chiapas did not become fully a part of Mexico until after independence in the 19th century.

The houses of San Cristóbal de las Casas have red tile roofs and walls of faded pastel colors, and iron grilles cover the windows. The sidewalks are high; there are big gutters and rainpipes jutting out over the street for the heavy rains. A big doorway usually opens on to an inner patio where family life goes on in full view. Hotels use this arrangement to create flowery courtyards where guests can read in the sun and sip their drinks. One of these hostelries was the home of Mazariegos. It can get cold at this altitude (2,262 m/7,465 ft), and many hotel rooms have fireplaces.

The Avenida General Utrilla will lead gently upward to the **Santo Domingo** church, a 16th- and 17th-century Baroque beauty of buff stone with leafy encrustations on its twisting columns. A quiet gathering of Indian women and their children sit under trees beside the church, weaving and selling their wares. The **Museo Etnografía y Historia** adjoining the church houses a rich exhibit of the textiles and embroidery patterns of Chiapas villages. Present-day examples of these same crafts are sold across the street at **Sna Jolobil** (Tzotzil for "house of weaving"), a cooperative representing the women of 20 villages dedicated to preserving traditional handwork. Along this street are shops selling men's belts of braided leather, fancy machetes, baskets made from armadillo armor, embroidered bags, sarapes, and wool rugs.

At the top of the rise, the mercado spreads out for many blocks in the open air around a market building. It is a refreshingly authentic scene, vivid with the costumes of the surrounding villages, the scents and colors of their produce, the squeals and squawks of their animals, and the sing-song sibilance of Tzotzil. Tourists are warned quite seriously not to photograph these Indians without their permission. Good photographs of the Indians are sold in book and postcard form at the **Casa Na Bolom** Center at the upper end of Calle Vicente Guerrero. They are taken by Gertrude Blom, a Swiss photographer-anthropologist-ecologist and widow of the Maya expert Frans Blom, who has made her house a base for scholars and archaeologists for many years. You may visit the library, collections, and shop. Don't leave town before a climb up **Cerro de San Cristóbal** (St. Christopher's Hill) to visit the church here and admire the fine view over the city.

Indian Villages of Chiapas

The nearby Indian villages certainly merit a detour and can be reached either by cab or colectivo. The best way to see the nearby

Baroque beauty: Santa Domingo Church commands pride of place in San Cristóbal de las Casas, Chiapas.

villages is to meet up with one of the three local tour guides who take small groups to the towns. These people are well informed about the customs of the towns, where the law of Mexico matters less than the law of the communities. Also, be careful about photographing; several tourists have been hurt by local men when they pulled out their cameras to take pictures. Mercedes Hernández leaves from the zócalo around 9am. Alex and Raul leave from here also, around 9.30am, and Pepe leaves from Casa Na-Bolom around 10am.

The village of **San Juan Chamula**, and its church especially, are must-sees. Inside, hundreds and hundreds of candles set on a floor carpeted with pine needles provide both light and heat. You may see men facing the altar with a bottle on the floor in front of them. From time to time they will take a swallow from their bottle – it is hard liquor, and the act is ritual drinking. This ceremony, rooted in the Maya past, is to "bring back the spirit" to a person who has lost his appetite for food or for life. The outward signs here are Christian, but Maya traditions lie just beneath the surface. It is forbidden to

photograph in the church or during the dancing at festivals. Outside, the men in capes carrying staffs are the elected guardians of the shrine. It is an honor to have this responsibility, or cargo, even though it is expensive – the cargo officers have to pay for the festivals during the year of their service. As a footnote to history, note that San Juan de Chamula and its environs were given to the chronicler of the conquest, Bernal Díaz del Castillo.

Zinacantán, about 5 km (3 miles) farther on, is a ceremonial center, also guarded by cargo officers. These villages are packed with dancers on feast days.

Mayan Indian children against a colorful backdrop of cloth in Zinacantán, Chiapas.

175

(Inquire at the Tourist Information Office in San Cristóbal de las Casas for dates and times.) Horseback rides from town can be arranged. It is pleasant to walk one way, past small farms and orchards, by streams where women are doing the wash and through stretches of woodland, and then ride the colectivo back in the other direction.

The closest airport to San Cristóbal de las Casas is in the Chiapas capital, Tuxtla Gutiérrez. The 90-minute trip passes through mountainous terrain where coffee and flowers are grown. Off go the sweaters as you drop down to 530 m (1,738 ft). Short side trips off this road worth considering are to **Chiapa de Corzo**, 16 km (10 miles) outside Tuxtla Gutiérrez. This very old village is famous for its lacquered masks and gourds, which are sold around the zócalo and in the shop of the small Museo de la Laca. The dammed Rio Grijalva backs up into a lake and the spectacular narrow **Cañón del Sumidero**, with walls more than 1,000 m (3,000 ft) high. You can ride a boat down the gorge and back from Chiapa de Corzo in a couple of hours, or view the fjord-like scenery from El Sumidero lookout on a road from Tuxtla Gutiérrez. (There are in fact two airports in Tuxtla Gutiérrez, one 25 minutes out of town and the other closer in. Which one is operating depends on the time of year. Be sure to find out which one your plane is leaving from.)

THE GULF COAST

Veracruz

Veracruz isn't on most tourist itineraries. Its residents tend to be unaffected, unbuttoned, and very sure of themselves. They have a good time and will make room for visitors to share the fun, but don't make a big business of it. Veracruz has the best Carnival and maybe the worst handicraft market. It is steeped in history, but has few monuments. It was here that Cortés landed and burned his boats, here that Spanish dominion in Mexico ended three centuries later. The gold and silver galleons sailed for Spain from Veracruz, so it was a prime target for pirates. American marines and French *zouaves* invaded too. Today, as Mexico's principal seaport, the harbor is always filled with ships and the tooting of tugboats.

This is the background to keep in mind in Veracruz, but once you're here, the atmosphere will take over: just *being* here becomes more important than *doing* something. A lot of time can be passed happily just sitting in a café, listening to the special beat of local music, and imagining Humphrey Bogart, unshaven and in a stained white linen, making a deal with a shifty-eyed Peter Lorre at the next table. It's the archetypal tropical port you've seen in a hundred movies.

A look at the city could begin with a walk along the harborside promenade, the Malecón, which is called "El Boulevard" after it turns away from the harbor and runs south along the coast. Next to the Malecón is a plaza with a Stalinesque statue of President Venustiano Carranza, who briefly made Veracruz the capital of Mexico in 1914, and across the plaza stands a former lighthouse of the Carranza period. On the Malecón's broad esplanade tickets are sold for the boat ride out around the harbor and around the **Isla de Sacrificios**, the lighthouse island where some remains of sacrifices have been found. The short trip gives a breezy view of the city from the sea.

The **Mercado de Curiosidades** is at the very beginning of the Malecón. It is rightfully called the market of curios, for the crafts tend to tacky knickknacks made of seashells, cheap scarves, and plastic ship models. Across the street, on the Insurgentes section of the Malecón, ceiling fans stir the air in a block-long café as big as a bus station. This is **Café de la Parroquia**, an institution in this city, packed to overflowing at meal-times. Breakfast is especially nice to have here. Order a *café lechero* (coffee with milk) and you'll be served a glass with a couple of jiggers of strong black coffee at the bottom. Tap it with your spoon to get the attention of the waiters who circulate with kettles of hot foaming milk, which they pour with a great flourish.

Castello San Juan de Ulúa, the most interesting historical monument in Veracruz lies across the harbor. You can ride out by boat from the Malecón, or take a bus from a stop just to the north of the Palacio Municipal to this fortification, now surrounded by the cranes and tracks of a container-ship dock and rail terminal. Built in the mid-18th century on the site of 16th-century fortifications, the bastion was the last Spanish foothold in Mexico. The Spanish fleet bombarded independence forces in Veracruz in 1822, when royalist refugees filled the fort. It finally surrendered to a young Mexican officer named Santa Anna making his first mark on history.

The castle-fortress and its predecessors seem to have done little to protect Veracruz. The English privateers Sir Francis Drake and John Hawkins took and retook the city in the late 1500s, and Dutch freebooter Laurent de Graff, feared around the Gulf as "Lorencillo," sacked and burned it for three days in 1683. The French bombarded the city twice, and the US three times, in 1847, 1914, and 1917. Small wonder that few monuments are left. In the 19th century San Juan de Ulúa was a notoriously horrible prison, with walls 2½ m (8 ft) thick and the sea for a moat. Carranza turned the prison headquarters into a presidential residence, but was assassinated before he could occupy it.

The **Museo Regional**, at 397 Calle Zaragoza, is worth visiting to sort out the turbulent history of the town. This is the only museum that documents the role of African slaves in Mexico. Cortés imported the first from Cape Verde to work his sugar plantations and in 1641 records showed 35,089 Africans in New Spain. Communities founded by escaped slaves near Acapulco still have a strong African strain and the Cuban-African influence in music and race is marked around Veracruz. A pronouncement abolishing slavery was one of the first acts of Father Hidalgo during the uprising of 1810, but slaves were not actually freed until the constitution of 1857.

The museum also has a small section about the pirates' attacks against the city and another on the epidemics that savaged Veracruz for

A woman enters into the spirit of the occasion, at the famously spectacular Carnival celebrations in Veracruz.

much of its history, such as yellow fever and malaria. Another museum close by is installed in the **Baluarte de Santiago**, a remnant of the once formidable but ineffectual city battlements. Another is the **Museo de Historia Naval**, housed in the former naval academy, where you can get free guided tours that explain a lot of Veracruz's history as a port. The Acuario (aquarium) is one of the city's major attractions.

The heart of Veracruz is the **Plaza de Armas**, perhaps the most lively square in the nation. It is at its liveliest at night when the air is cool and families come out to stroll around. In front of the brightly lit Moorish-style city hall, the city's *danzonera* band starts playing at 8pm on Tuesdays, Thursdays, and Saturdays. Couples dance the *danzón* on the elevated platform that many years ago held a band-

stand similar to other plazas. The **danzón** is traditional in the port of Veracruz. It was brought here from Cuba in the last century, and Veracruzanos have made it their own. In it, couples alternate between a rumba-like dance and short promenades, during which the women wave beautiful hand-held fans. Soon after the danzón one can hear different styles of music as itinerant musicians strike up their tunes – mariachi and ranchero, which now might be considered Mexico's national music; or Jarocha, from the region just south of the port, from which originated *La Bamba*; or marimba, which probably came from Chiapas via Tabasco and now much-loved here. Veracruzanos actually like any music that is cheerful and rhythmic, such as salsa. The goings on in the plaza can last until 3am.

Take a table at one of the cafés under the arches, order the food and beverage of your choice, and sit back and watch the goings-on. Without moving from your table you have the opportunity to buy locally made or Cuban cigars, lottery tickets, seafood, articles of clothing, sunglasses, and the ubiquitous chiclets. Most of the people in the surrounding tables will be locals, and you can see how well they enjoy themselves. With all the hoopla, it's as if Carnival had never stopped.

Carnival, of course, is the main event of the year for the city. Hotel reservations have to be made well in advance. It is particularly popular with people from other parts of Mexico who view Veracruz society as being much less rigid and inhibited than society in the rest of the country. Carnival in Veracruz is for them an opportunity to go a little crazy. It begins on the Tuesday before Ash Wednesday in the zócalo with the burning of the effigy of *Mal Humor* (bad humor) and ends with the symbolic burial of "Juan Carnival," accompanied by a morality play on the evils of drink and infidelity. Clubs work all year long on their costumes, bands, and floats for parades.

At El Tajín, workers tend to the land while an important Totonac archeological site looms in the background.

The Coast

Gulf Coast beaches aren't all that fantastic. The best at Veracruz is **Mocambo**, a resort with hotel gardens, pools, and restaurants on a very broad flat beach. The water is shallow a long way out. Farther on are **Boca del Río** and **Mandinga**, villages abounding in seafood restaurants and bars where *La Bamba* and similar *jarocha* songs are accompanied by the Veracruz "harp" and guitars. "Authentic" and "seedy" are adjectives equally appropriate to these popular weekend retreats.

The spot where Cortés landed on 22 April 1519 is unmarked but presumed to be facing the little island of San Juan de Ulúa. The day was Good Friday; he later optimistically named his base **La Villa Rica de la Vera Cruz**, the "Rich Town of the True Cross." That base was moved several times, finally to the present city limits. The first town, just to the north, is now a village of cobbled streets, **La Antigua**, where the only monument is a bust of the national hero, Benito Juárez. About 40 km (25 miles) north, off Route 180, are the ruins of **Zempoala**, the **Totonac** city where Cortés recruited allies that were to be crucial to his battles with the Aztecs. There are five partly reconstructed pyramid-temples and bits and pieces of Totonac buildings throughout the modern town. On weekends you are likely to find the famous *voladores* who come here from Papantla (see page 184).

Into the Mountains

The coastal hinterland between Veracruz and Villahermosa is the cradle of Mexican civilization, the home of the Olmecs from 1200 to around 400 B.C. Little has survived of the cities they built of wood and mud brick in swampy, almost inaccessible areas. But the Olmecs left amazing works of art and influenced the cultures that followed.

To see a superb collection of these treasures, it is worth making the 96-km (60-mile) trip to the state capital, **Xalapa** (*ha-LA-pa*,

Age-old tradition continues here in El Tajín, as villagers perform a dance in honor of the sun.

often spelled Jalapa). The road, which eventually reaches Puebla, winds up into cool highlands where you'll get a good view of the perpetual snows and perfect cone of the **Pico de Orizaba**, at 5,700 m (18,551 ft) the highest mountain in Mexico. Azaleas and camellias bloom in January in this cool mountain city of attractive, lush gardens. The light drizzle of the *chipi-chipi* rains keeps it refreshingly green.

The beautiful modern **Museo de Arqueología**, a work of art in itself, is one of the most important in Mexico. In addition to the Olmec collection, it has a vast collection of the Totonac and Huastec cultures. The pieces that get the most attention, however, are six of the huge Olmec basalt "helmeted" heads. They seem to have been transported to the Olmec cities at San Lorenzo, Tres Zapotes, and La Venta, probably by raft, as far as 128 km (80 miles) from the nearest quarry. Just as remarkable, the finely chiseled portraits were cut in the hard stone without metal tools. Yet after such effort, the heads were deliberately disfigured by the Olmecs and buried in the pits.

The Olmecs worshipped a Jaguar God. Many figures in the museum are of a fanged half-human, half-animal "were-jaguar." A particularly moving sculpture is of a priest holding in his lap the limp body of a sacrificed child. Other sculptures show a realism that represents a departure from the Olmec stylization. Also exhibited are the four-wheeled animal toys in clay; figures with the artificially deformed heads copied by the Maya; superb portraits in terracotta, some painted and with holes in the head for inserting hair or feathers; and a model of a ball game that shows that this ritual, too, originated with the Olmecs. There are also many of the curious laughing boys with flat triangular faces that belong to the Totonac culture. Surely this is one of the greatest museums of its kind. It is open 9am–5pm, closed Monday.

The Xalapa museum contains a number of works from the Totonac city **El Tajín** in the northern part of the state. The remarkable feature of this important ruin is the **Templo de los Niches**, a six-layered pyramid, pierced by closely set window-like niches. The architecture of all the buildings at this large site is unlike anything else in Mexico. Some of the Totonac pottery boasts scroll designs and tripod feet that are very much like Chinese vessels.

El Tajín is a few miles from **Papantla**, the vanilla-growing hometown of the *voladores*, the men who go spinning around at the end of long ropes hanging from a tall pole. Since they perform all over the country, one need not make the day-long round trip from Veracruz to see them on their native ground. But it is too bad that El Tajín is so far off the beaten track, for it is well worth a visit. North of this region is the oil-producing and shipping area around Tampico and Poza Rica, and then the long road to the Texas border at Matamoros-Brownsville.

WHAT TO DO

SPORTS AND OUTDOOR ACTIVITIES

Whether you are a sportsman or spectator, golfer or surfer, Mexico is a natural playground for the actively inclined.

All resorts have **tennis** courts that are in excellent condition. Some hotels offer lighted and covered courts, with a variety of surfaces that include clay and grass. Among the resort areas with the best tennis facilities are Puerto Vallarta, on the Pacific Coast, and Loreto, on the Sea of Cortez. In Puerto Vallarta the tennis aficionado will find two top-class tennis centers. The Continental Plaza Tennis Club, located in the Hotel Continental Plaza in the hotel zone, offers eight courts, four covered and four clay, with courts open daily 7am

Mexico offers plenty of options for an activity-filled vacation, but if you simply feel like lounging by the pool, you won't be alone!

–10pm; Tel. (322) 224-0123, ext. 500. The Iguana Tennis Center, located just off the highway before the entrance to Marina Vallarta, has three courts, one outdoor and two covered with Astroturf surfaces, open daily 9am–9pm; Tel. (322) 221-0683. In Loreto, you can play tennis at the Centro Tenístico Loreto– also known as the John McEnroe Tennis Center – adjacent to the Eden Resort, with nine lighted asphalt courts; Tel. (613) 133-0408. Court fees across Mexico range between 75 and 180 pesos per hour. Most tennis courts offer rentals ranging between 25 and 50 pesos per raquet.

Golfers will find courses in good to excellent condition in almost every resort and all major cities in Mexico. Most golf courses have carts and clubs for rent, should you prefer to travel light. Los Cabos has become the country's golf Mecca, for its world class courses that are equal or superior to those found in other countries, not only for the quality of the courses, but also for the scenery they offer. Los Cabos currently boasts five championship courses, with more on the drawing board: the Palmilla Golf Club; Tel. (624) 144-5021 and Cabo del Sol Resort Golf Course; Tel. (624) 145-8200, were both designed by Jack Nicklaus; the Cabo Real Golf Club; Tel. (624) 144-0040, was designed by Robert Trent Jones II; the Campo de Golf San José, owned by FONATUR (Mexico's Tourism Fund); Tel. (624) 142-0900, and the Cabo San Lucas Country Club; Tel. (624) 143-4653, were designed by the Dye group. Green fees in Cabos range between 300 and 2,500 pesos. An annual roster of tournaments includes the PGA Senior Slam, held each year in early spring.

The northern Pacific coast offers several championship courses between Puerto Vallarta and Manzanillo, all in excellent condition with exceptional coastal views and uncrowded greens and fairways. A new Jack Nicklaus course, just north of Puerto Vallarta at the Four Seasons Punta Mita, has a spectacular hole that drives to a natural island 175 yards offshore; Tel. (322) 291-6035. The Bay of Banderas, where Puerto Vallarta is located, will soon offer a total of six courses, including the public course at Club de Golf Flamingos; Tel. (322) 298-0280, and the Marina Vallarta Golf Club; Tel. (322) 221-0545, designed by Joe Finger. Going south along the coastline, known as the Costa Alegre, spectacular courses offer exclusive play and oceanside vistas at Isla Navidad; Tel. (322) 355-5556, one of Mexico's top rated resort courses designed by Robert Von Hagge, and El Tamarindo; Tel. (322) 551-5031, designed by David Fleming. American Golf Tours; Tel. (322) 225-2056, and Best Golf; Tel. 1-800-817 GOLF, offer information on all of these regional golf courses, where green fees range between 400 and 1600 pesos per 18 holes. In Manzanillo, golf is an almost essential part of the Las Hadas resort, where La Mantarray golf course; Tel. (314) 334-0000, designed by Roy and Pete Dye, is considered among the most scenic in the world, with its million dollar island green on the 18th hole. Green fees on these courses range between 750 and 1200 pesos.

Punta Sur, the southernmost point of Isla Mujeres, offers big waves – and big fish, too!

Scuba diving and **snorkeling** on the Caribbean reefs are world-class, with Cozumel, Isla Mujeres, and Cancún being the most popular spots for year-round underwater activities. Cozumel is one of the top ten dive destinations in the world. The mainland side of the island offers the best diving, both in the national park at Palancar and in other dive sites such as Columbia, Paraíso, and the spectacular wall dive at Santa Rosa. For more experienced divers, Maracaibo and Barracuda offer incredible sights and spectacular coral formations starting at 25 m (80 ft). Several of the sites for shallow dives, especially Palancar, Paraíso, and Columbia, are also ideal for snorkeling, with parts of the reef coming within 1 m (3 ft) of the surface. Most dive shops offer resort courses and full-fledge certification courses for those who can't wait to enjoy the underwater beauty of the place. One of Cozumel's longest standing dive-shops offering tours and instruction is Aquaworld; Tel. (987) 872-1210.

Isla Mujeres has good sites, with Manchones reef (1 km/½ mile out) being the closest. Manchones is also ideal for snorkeling, because of its shallow waters (between 5 and 11 m/15 and 35 ft) and great visibility. Another excellent site for snorkeling is the Lighthouse Reef just off the northwestern tip of the island, and if you want to snorkel from the shore there is the El Garrafón/Punta Sur national park encompassing the island's southern tip. The most extraordinary diving experience from Isla Mujeres is the cave of the sleeping sharks, where, between January and March, you can see nurse sharks floating and very still inside a sea cave. The dive shop with the longest-standing reputation on Isla Mujeres is Buzos de México; Tel. (998) 877-0500; Sea Friends, located right on Playa Norte, is another good option; Tel. (998) 842-5348.

Cancún is a true haven for beginner divers and snorkelers, with numerous shallow dive sites. Punta Nizuc is the best site for diving in Cancún. It is also the northern tip of the Gran Arrecife Maya, the largest reef in the Western Hemisphere, extending south past Cozumel and Belize. The largest operator in Cancún, also offering

Catch of the day: deep sea fishing is excellent along the Pacific coast. Marlin, yellowtail, and tuna are all plentiful.

resort courses and off-shore dives, is Aquaworld; Tel. (998) 885-2288. Experienced divers can enjoy the unique experience of cenote diving in fresh water springs with cave formations; with access to snorkelers as well, the largest cavern system is just north of Tulum; contact Hidden Worlds on Tel. (984) 877-8535.

The Pacific coast waters offer their own treasures, with extraordinary dive sites off the shores of Los Cabos and Cabo Pulmo. Here divers can enter an amazing submarine world where the spectacle of the sand falls brings to mind the constant movement of the continental plates, and encounters with sea-lions, dolphins, and even whale-sharks are part of the daily adventure. Most hotels and resorts offer reputable dive shops with certified divers and instructors.

Deep sea fishing is excellent along the Pacific coast. Mazatlán has a reputation for being one the best spots for marlin, tuna, and yellowtail. Several fleets offer their services to avid fishermen from

all over the world. The best season is October–January; rates go from around 1,600 pesos for a small outboard boat called a *panga* to close to 3,000 pesos for a private fishing charter on a 12½-m (38-ft) cruiser. It is best to contact an established fleet recommended by the tourism office in Mazatlán; Tel. (669) 916-5160.

Sea-kayaking along the coastal inlets and islands of the Sea of Cortez is increasing in popularity. The best areas are concentrated near La Paz and Loreto. In La Paz, contact Las Parras Tours (Tel. 1/135-1010), or Fenton's Sea Kayaking (Tel. 1/135-3407). Both offer kayak lessons and tours than range in length from half a day to overnight. Loreto offers sea-kayaking island exploration tours for beginning, intermediate, and advanced kayakers. The tour can be customized to fit your needs and expectations, including camping by moonlight on deserted islands. Las Parras also offers the widest variety of sea-kayaking tours in Loreto, plus excellent advice regarding other outdoor activities in the area. It is easy to find operators offering waterskis, windsurfing boards, parasailing, and noisy little wave-runners on the beaches of most hotels.

Puerto Escondido has one of the best **surfing** beaches in the world, and there's good surfing at San Blas as well. The best waves along the Mexican coast are caught during the fall. Puerto Escondido has several economical inns that welcome surfers from all over the world. San Blas has a much smaller tourism infrastructure. Surfers seem to have their own network for sources of information regarding the best beaches and hang-outs, so word-of-mouth is the best way to learn all the secrets for the best beaches and waves. Another good option is to contact Tropical Surf in Cruz de Juanacaxtle; Tel. (329) 295-5087.

Eco- and adventure tourism are becoming increasingly popular in Mexico, where the rugged, varied terrain of the lanscape provides

Parachute into Acapulco, catch a wave at Puerto Escondido – whatever your sport, Mexico can likely oblige.

Locals love charreadas, a Mexican version of a rodeo. Organized by horsemen's clubs, they are held on Sundays at noon.

the perfect backdrop for such adventures. With more tourists looking for these options, the Mexican Association of Adventure Travel and Ecotourism (AMTAVE) offers the most complete information about ecotourism and adventure tours, with close to 40 travel providers as members; website <www.amtave.com>. As a rule, in Mexico there are no marked trails or ranger stations as you commonly find in the US and Europe, and it is therefore better to go to a local operator or contact a company in the US or Europe that can help you arrange an outing that suits your ability and sense of adventure.

Hiking and backpacking in the Copper Canyon area take you into real wilderness; the best way to enjoy these wonderful and physically demanding trails is to hire an experienced guide or contact an organizer to arrange transportation, lodging, and hiking through some of the most scenic areas. Naturequest (Tel. in the US 949/499-9561; website <www.naturequesttours.com>) and Wildland Adventures (Tel. in the US 800-345-4453; website <www.wildland.com>) are two companies with excellent options for serious hikers and backpackers.

The Sierra Madre Mountains adjacent to Puerto Vallarta offer challenging and easily accessible **hiking** and **mountain biking** excursions. Bike-Mex offers expert guided tours into the mountains and other outlying areas; Tel. (322) 223-1834. Biking in Baja, with an accompanying van to carry your luggage, is becoming popular. The American Wilderness Experience offers this kind of trip and other options for personally designed trips in Baja; Tel. in the US (303) 444-2622 or 800-444-0099. Take part in a thrilling rafting excursion or kayak down the gorge of the Usumacinta River, or the numerous rivers in the state of Veracruz. In Jalapa, Veraventuras offers the most options for rafting along the different rivers in the state, with tours for all expertise levels; Tel. in Xalapa (228) 818-9779; website <www.veraventures.com.mx>. For information about trips to the Usumacinta river, call the state of Chiapas tourism office; Tel. (961) 678-0665.

Spectator Sports

There's **greyhound racing** every day at Agua Caliente in Tijuana and **horse racing** Friday, Saturday and Sunday in Mexico City. Betting is also part of the excitement in Acapulco, at the courts called *frontones*, where jai-alai is played. In this lightning-fast Basque version of handball, players whip the ball with wicker scoops strapped to their hands.

Charreadas, a Mexican kind of **rodeo** organized by horsemen's clubs, are held almost every Sunday noon at several rings in Mexico City, in Guadalajara, and on occasion in other cities of the north. In

A matador struts his stuff at a corrida in Tizimín. Bullfighting remains a popular spectator sport in Mexico.

Mexico City, the Corrida de Toros, or **bullfighting**, takes place October–March in the world's largest ring, the 42,000-seat Plaza Mexico, off Insurgentes Sur. The program starts punctually at 4pm on Sunday. For ticket information, go to the Plaza on Saturday morning, or call; Tel. (55) 5563-3961. The livelier crowd sits in the sunny section *sección de sol*; however, the seats in the covered section are cooler in the afternoon sun. If you really want to feel the excitement of the corrida, splurge and get *barrera* tickets – these are the closest to the ring, but note that they are not for those who have any mixed feelings about the Fiesta Brava. In barreras you hear the bull, you smell the blood, and you taste the dust from the ring as the bull charges. From June or July–September are the *novilladas* in which up-and-coming bullfighters match their wits against smaller bulls. Tickets to charreadas and bullfights are often part of a tour, or can be bought through a travel agency.

SHOPPING

The best shopping in Mexico is for handcrafted artesanía, decorative objects, and, due to the presence of rich mineral mines of Mexico's mountains, silver jewelry. Each region in Mexico has its own specialties; in each, artisan traditions are handed down from generation to generation and blend the area's unique mix of indigenous and Spanish roots.

Best Buys

The following is a partial list of articles that are uniquely and charmingly Mexican:

Handcrafted and Decorative Objects

Pottery of all kinds, glazed and often painted in designs unique to each locale; hand-blown glassware from Jalisco state; naïve paintings on bark or stitched in yarn from Morelos and Nayarit; wildly exuberant Adam and Eve "Tree of Life" candelabra from the states of Mexico and Puebla; grotesque masks used in traditional indigenous ceremonies; whimsical, colorful animals made of carved wood and papier maché, called Alebrijes, from Oaxaca; exquisite lacquerware from Olinala, in Guerrero and Michoacán; and straw products, from baskets to Panama-style hats, found in coastal regions. Basketry is also a specialty in the Copper Canyon area.

Found across the country are wood-carved boxes; toys and Christmas tree ornaments in painted tin; nutshells housing tiny figures and miniature doll furniture; maracas made from gourds that are carved, painted, and lacquered; and piñatas, the candy-filled papier-maché balloons in fanciful shapes.

For the collector, genuine colonial antiques can be found, as well as excellent copies. Mexico City's Bazaar Sabado is an excellent place to search.

Silver and Jewelry

Silver jewelry, picture frames, and ornaments can be a bargain (but buy only those with the "925" stamp, denoting true silver). There are beautifully crafted vessels of copper, plus mirrors, lanterns, and chandeliers of ornamental tin.

Mexican opals, turquoise, lapis lazuli, onyx, and other semi-precious stones and minerals are downright cheap. Mexico's silver capital is Taxco, but shops throughout the country feature fine Mexican silver.

Handicraft Items

Fine, hand-loomed woolen sarapes (a kind of poncho), from Saltillo and Oaxaca; cotton, wool, or silk shawls of many colors, called rebozos, from San Luis Potosí; rugs in Indian designs; huipiles, the square-cut embroidered blouses worn by indigenous women throughout Mexico; and guayaberas, box-cut men's shirts, with pleats and some embroidery, made popular in the Yucatán, Campeche, Tabasco, and Veracruz.

Leather goods such as huarache sandals, belts, jackets, wallets, handbags, and hats are especially popular in Leon and

Mexico City's Bazar del Sábado is the perfect place to hunt for Mexican arts and crafts.

197

MARKETS

Here are some places with markets selling typical crafts. When bargaining, keep in mind that a 30 percent reduction of the original offer is usually a fair price for the vendor, though most travelers will find that even full price represents a bargain compared to prices in the US and Europe. Markets are generally open every day except Sunday, from around 9am–6pm. Market days – when people from the surrounding areas come to sell their wares – are noted in parenthesis, where appropriate.

Mexico City

Bazar del Sábado. *Plaza San Jacinto, San Ángel.* Saturdays 9am–6pm (see page 68).

FONART. *Avenida Juárez 89, Centro Histórico by the Alameda; Tel. (5) 521-0171.* Monday–Saturday 10am–7pm. Metro Hidalgo.

La Lagunilla. *Rayon and Allende, Centro.* Daily 9am–6pm; flea market with antiques on Allende street Saturdays 10am–6pm. Metro Garibaldi.

Mercado de Artesanías de la Ciudadela. *Balderas and Ayuntamiento.* Daily 9am–6pm. Metro Juárez.

Mercado de Artesanías de San Juan *Ayuntamiento and Izazaga, Centro Histórico.* Daily 9am–6pm. Metro Juárez.

Mercado de Sonora. *Fray Servando T. de Mier and La Viga, Centro.* Daily 9am–6pm. Metro Merced.

Elsewhere

Acapulco: Sportswear, all-Mexico shopping, regional candies made of coconut and tamarind, ceramics, bark paintings.

Acatlán (Puebla): Tree of Life candlesticks, ceramics (Sunday).

Chiapa de Corzo (Chiapas): Lacquered gourds, masks, huipiles.

Cuernavaca: Bark paintings, baskets, silver, herbs (Sunday).

Coyotepec (Oaxaca): Black pottery.

Copper Canyon: Tarahumara baskets, hats, violins, pottery.

Guadalajara: Glassware, silver, charro hats, pottery, tooled leather goods (piteados).

Guanajuato: Silver, gold, minerals, skeleton candy and toys.

Jocotepec (Lake Chapala): White embroidered sarapes (Sunday).

Mérida: Huipiles and guayaberas, hammocks, Panama hats, huaraches, gold.

Metepec (Estado de México): Candlesticks (Monday).

Morelia: Green pottery, woodwork, straw figures, masks, laquered woodwork (Sunday).

Mitla (Oaxaca): Rebozos, sarapes (Thursday).

Oaxaca: Baskets, pottery, wrought iron, rebozos, sarapes, huipiles (Saturday).

Ocotlán (Oaxaca): Baskets, sarapes, rugs, leather (Friday).

Olinalá (Guerrero): Lacquered chests and boxes.

Paracho (Michoacán): Guitars, violins.

Pátzcuaro: Ceramics, lacquer, embroidery, baskets (Friday).

Puebla: Ceramics, onyx, embroidery, tiles, saddles (Sunday).

Puerto Vallarta: Huaraches, jewelry, resort-wear, Huichol Indian and Latin American art.

Querétaro: Amethysts, opals.

Saltillo: Wool sarapes.

San Juan del Río: Opals, rebozos.

San Miguel de Allende: Tinware, ceramics, silver, mirrors.

San Cristóbal: Leather, bags, weaving, embroidery.

Santa Clara del Cobre (Michoacán): Copperware.

Taxco: Silver and gold jewelry.

Teotitlán del Valle (Oaxaca): Sarapes, wool rugs.

Tequisquiapan (Querétaro): Wicker and rattan furniture and accessories.

Tlacolula (Oaxaca): Pottery, embroidery, rugs (Sunday).

Tlaquepaque (Guadalajara): Pottery, furniture, glassware.

Uruapan: Lacquer boxes and trays, masks.

Zacatecas: Carved stone, silver.

Guadalajara. The tooled-leather saddles and boots are Mexican works of art, known as Piteado, and created in Jalisco.

Markets

Wherever you go in Mexico there will be a market, and in every market you will find local handicrafts (see pages 198–199). The government's handicrafts foundation (FONART) has shops at several locations in Mexico City and in major tourist centers. Representatives from FONART scour the countryside and buy direct from artisans in order to offer the highest quality at the fairest possible price. In Mexico City, the main location is on Patriotismo 691, open daily 9am–8pm; Tel. (55) 5598-1666 and a branch at Avenida Juarez 89, near the Alemeda, open Monday–Saturday 10am–7pm; Tel. (55) 5521-0171. Within Mexico's interior, you can find

Handwoven baskets make the ideal souvenir. A weaver at work in Chilapa, Guerrero State.

FONART stores in San Luis Potosí, Oaxaca, and Tlaquepaque.

The municipal and state governments also operate Mercados, Centros de Artesanías, and the fixed-price shops found in many museums around the country. If you want to take your shopping seriously, it's useful to check the prices, quality, and variety of goods in these places to compare for bargaining in the public markets and craft shops.

In the capital and resort areas such as Acapulco, Cancún, Puerto Vallarta, and Mazatlán, crafts from every part of the country are sold in the markets. This is good to know when you're grinding your teeth over a missed opportunity in Pátzcuaro or Oaxaca. But it's more fun to buy your finds from the source, all the more so to see them being made by village weavers and potters. You'll find more variety at the source, too, though prices won't be much lower. Increased demand resulting from mass tourism has definitely lowered standards. Shop around and don't hesitate to point out what competing shops and stalls are offering. You may find, too, that established handicraft shops, while costing more, offer better quality than the big *artesanía* markets.

Xochimilco has its share of wares, but for some the romance of the riverboat experience is indulgence enough!

A taste for the exotic? Try dinner on a "floating garden" restaurant in Xochimilco.

ENTERTAINMENT

Mexico's nightlife is as varied as the country's geography, and ranges from sizzling-hot Latin dance clubs to romantic *boleros* played in public plazas. The most dynamic entertainment is found in Mexico City and in the resort areas. The big city nightlight mirrors that of Spain, with clubs of live music and dancing staying open

very late, and night-owl cafés. In Cancún, the clubs are primarily predictable, world-renowned chains, located in grand entertainment and shopping centers. Cabo San Lucas, despite its recent gentrification, still maintains an outlaw-style nightlife, with a row of rowdy bars open until it's time to head out fishing again. In Puerto Vallarta, a respectable live music scene has emerged, with a collection of clubs in walking distance from one another that play everything from the Blues to Mariachi. No resort is better known for sizzling nightlife than Acapulco, with its dazzling cliffside discos and more casual but dynamic bars that line the waterfront along the main drag; you'll also find a healthy selection of Cuban salsa clubs, chorus lines of female impersonators, an active red-light district – it's all here.

Mexico City's Ballet Folklórico de México is an institution, and puts on a show that everyone wants to see at least once. The chance to see its home near the Alameda, the Palacio de Bellas Artes, with its Tiffany glass curtain of sunrise over the volcanoes and Valley of Mexico, is alone worth the price of admission. The program recreates pre-Hispanic dances as well as Mexico's wonderfully varied regional music and fiestas, with gorgeous costumes. An easy way to arrange tickets is through your hotel's travel agency – they will probably provide good seats and pick you up at your hotel. For tickets and information (in Spanish) call the Palacio de Bellas Artes; Tel. (55) 5512-2593. For advance purchase and delivery of tickets, call Ticketmaster, an electronic ticketing service; Tel. (55) 5325-9000. The ballet performs year-round on Wednesdays at 8.30pm and Sundays at 9.30am and 8.30pm. However, check with the office to confirm; the Sunday evening performance is frequently cancelled to accommodate other events.

Touring companies of the Ballet Folklórico perform fairly regularly in Acapulco, Cancún, and other cities. The provinces have quite good ballets of their own, too – Mérida's is one of the best. If you're in Oaxaca the last two Mondays in July, get tickets to the Guelaguetza, held in the amphitheatre on the Cerro del Fortín overlooking the city, in which dances of the state's seven regions are performed in native costumes, including the huge feather headdress of the Danza de las Plumas. Tickets are available through the state tourism office; Tel. (951) 516-0994 or (951) 514-2155. You should purchase your tickets well in advance in order to guarantee a space. Throughout Mexico, traditional entertainment accompanies all major holidays and the innumerable local fiestas. And every resort hotel worth the salt on its margarita glasses has a "Fiesta Mexicana" night at least once a week.

Beautiful turn-of-the-century theaters have been restored in the Silver Cities (see page 86) and Oaxaca. Concerts, opera, musical comedy, and stage plays are performed regularly in these gilt-and-velvet halls. Important cultural festivals, such as the October Cervantes Festival in Guanajuato, attract artists from around the world. This festival brings together performances of theater; classical, modern, and folkloric dance; and classical, folkloric, jazz, and rock concerts, featuring an international roster of talent. The city itself becomes the stage, with venues in all the plazas, theaters, and streets. The cultural institutions of San Miguel de Allende, Guadalajara, Cuernavaca, Puebla, and Morelia frequently schedule concerts and other performances that you will probably enjoy even if you don't speak Spanish. Check the English-language *Mexico City News* and local tourist information offices for details.

For informal entertainment, go to the *zócalo* in any city or town any evening around 8pm – especially on Sundays – and you'll probably find a band or a marimba orchestra up in the bandstand going all out for an appreciative crowd. Often there will be dancing. In Mérida a regular schedule of varied musical performances takes place in a different plaza every night. In Veracruz, the music goes on from mid-morning until late at night, with couples frequently danc-

Mexicans love nothing more than a fiesta, or any kind of street spectacle. Here, vibrance is the key, imagination the only limit.

Calendar of Events

New Year's Day. National holiday with parades, religious observances, parties, and fireworks everywhere.

Three Kings Day, 6 January. Children are given gifts to commemorate the Three Kings' bringing of gifts to the Christ Child.

Candlemas, 2 February. Music, dances, processions, food, and other festivities lead up to a blessing of seed and candles in a tradition that mixes pre-Hispanic and European traditions marking the end of winter.

Carnaval. Celebrated with revelry the three days preceding Ash Wednesday and the beginning of Lent. Carnaval is celebrated with special gusto in the cities of Tepoztlán, Huejotzingo, Chamula, Veracruz, Cozumel, and Mazatlán.

Benito Juárez's birthday, 21 March. Small hometown celebrations countrywide, especially in Juárez's birthplace – Guelatao, in Oaxaca state.

Spring Equinox, 21 March, Chichén-Itza. On the first day of spring, the Temple of Kukulcan aligns with the sun and the shadow of the plumed serpent moves slowly from the top of the building down, and visitors from afar come to marvel at this sight.

Holy Week. All of Mexico celebrates the last week in the life of Christ, from Palm Sunday–Easter Sunday. Businesses close during this traditional week of Mexican national vacations.

San Marcos national fair, Aguascalientes. Mexico's largest fair begins the third week in April and lasts 22 days.

Labor Day, 1 May. Workers parade countrywide and everything closes.

Cinco de Mayo, 5 May. A national holiday that celebrates the defeat of the French at the Battle of Puebla.

National Ceramics Fair and Fiesta, second week in June, Tlaquepaque. This pottery center on the outskirts of Guadalajara offers craft demonstrations, competitions, and more.

The Guelaguetza Dance Festival, last two Mondays in July, Oaxaca. One of Mexico's most popular events.

International Chamber Music Festival, 1–15 August, San Miguel de Allende. Held for more than 20 years, the festival features international award-winning classical music ensembles.

Fall of Tenochtitlán, 13 August, Mexico City. Wreath-laying ceremonies in the Plaza de las Tres Culturas commemorate the event when the last Aztec king, Cuauhtémoc, surrendered to Hernán Cortés and thousands lost their lives.

Mariachi Festival, 1–15 September, Guadalajara, Jalisco. Public concerts of mariachi music performed by groups from around the world, plus workshops and lectures on the history, culture, and music of the mariachi in Mexico.

Independence Day, 15–16 September. Celebrates Mexico's independence from Spain with parades, picnics, and fiestas throughout the country. At 11pm on 15 September, the president of Mexico gives the famous independence grito (shout) from the national palace in Mexico City.

Autumnal Equinox, 21 September, Chichén-Itzá. The same shadow play that occurs during the spring equinox repeats itself for the fall equinox.

Cervantino Festival, early to mid-October, Guanajuato. This cultural event attracts performing artists from all over the world.

Fiestas de Octubre (October Festivals), Guadalajara. This "most Mexican of cities" celebrates for a whole month with popular culture, fine arts, and mariachi music.

Days of the Dead. All Saints' Day, 1 November, honors saints and deceased children, while All Souls' Day, 2 November, honors deceased adults. Relatives gather at cemeteries with candles and food, often spending the night beside graves of loved ones.

Fiesta del Mar, Puerto Vallarta. A month-long calendar of activities includes art festivals, sports competitions, the Mexico boat show, and a gourmet dining festival.

National Silver Fair, 29 November to 6 December, Taxco. Exhibits, concerts, and fireworks commemorate Mexico's best silversmiths and some of the worlds finest artisans.

Feast of the Virgin of Guadalupe, 12 December. The patron saint of Mexico is honored with religious processions, street fairs, dancing, fireworks, and mass.

Christmas. Mexicans extend this celebration and leave their jobs often beginning two weeks before Christmas all the way through New Year's. Querétaro has a huge parade, while Oaxaca celebrates with its "Night of the Radishes," with displays of huge carved radishes.

New Year's Eve. The traditional parties, fireworks, and festivities are as they are the world over.

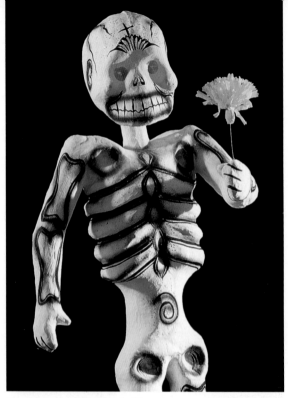

Days of the Dead: You may find it moving or merely macabre, but nowhere else is death as much a part of life as in Mexico.

ing the sultry *danzón* in the Plaza de Armas and the Parque Zamora.

The Plaza Garibaldi in Mexico City and Plaza de los Mariachis in Guadalajara seem never to sleep, with mariachi music playing non-stop. The mariachis congregate here and play, in an attempt to be hired out for a party. The atmosphere is festive, and it's a great way to hear a makeshift concert of this traditional music.

Fiestas

Somewhere in Mexico, you can be sure that a fiesta is underway right now. This has to be true, if only because every occupation and day of the year has a patron saint, because everybody has a birthday to share with neighbors and friends, because the seasons and the stars have always demanded recognition of their changes. Oaxaca even has a "Night of the Radishes," on 23 December, when the zócalo is surrounded by stalls of long red radishes carved into figures. Where but in Mexico do families stage an all-night vigil by the grave of a departed beloved while picnicking and eating skull-shaped candies? The famed Day of the Dead (Día de los Muertos) festivities take place throughout this land that seems to mock death in its accepted belief of an afterlife, but nowhere is it more visually moving than in the villages surrounding Pátzcuaro.

Mexico celebrates, with varying degrees of intensity, 13 official national holidays and 352 unofficial ones. Add one more for Leap Year. And don't count on the unofficial ones being celebrated on the same day each year – if a fiesta falls in midweek, some towns might decide to have the party on the weekend.

None of the national holidays has religious significance, with the exception of Christmas and Easter. Yet all the most important fiestas follow the Roman Catholic calendar. A celebration that begins with mass at the church may move into the plaza afterwards as masked dancers carry on ancient Indian rites. Only anthropologists really care about such matters – for participants a fiesta is a fiesta: a time for dressing up, marching in parades, decorating the zócalo with strings of lights or garlands of paper, setting off fireworks, eating, drinking, dancing, and being together with the whole family. In most cases, visitors can join the fray, but in some Indian villages, photography of rites is not allowed and onlookers should watch discreetly.

EATING OUT

Mexican cuisine rates as one of the world's most varied and unusual. It is a cuisine with many regional variations, but a number of generalities can be made about it. The first thing to note is that Mexican food relies on the same basic ingredients used in Pre-Columbian times: corn, beans, a wide variety of peppers (called chiles), tomatoes, squash, and avocado.

The corn is boiled with lime, allowed to sit, then drained, rinsed, and ground into a dough (*masa*). This masa is made into *tortillas* by pressing it into very thin circles and cooking it on a hot, seasoned griddle – usually a large, concave pan called a *comal*. The masa can also be formed into thicker cakes and cooked on the griddle, then opened and stuffed. Or, the masa can be combined with other ingredients and wrapped and steamed to make *tamales*. Tamales are an excellent example of regional variation. In northern Mexico and Texas they are small, have a lot of meat in them, and are wrapped in a corn husk. In central Mexico, they are larger and have a lot more masa that has been worked until it is very light. In the Huasteca region, tamales are so big that one can feed a family of eight. In Michoacán, they make a tamale that has no filling and is wrapped in a corn leaf, and another that is made of fresh corn rather than dried corn. In southern Mexico, they are wrapped in banana leaves and spiced with herbs not used elsewhere.

> **For a full meal at a low price, ask about the *comida corrida* or *menú del día*, usually offered between 2 and 4pm.**

Beans are cooked and served with the main course or afterwards. They are cooked with little seasoning because they are meant to provide contrast with the spiciness of the other dishes. In Mexican

Fruits and vegetables make for a colorful display at this market in Toluca.

Follow your nose: A woman sells freshly baked comal bread at an Ocotlán, Oaxaca market.

households, once the pot of beans has been around for a couple of days, the beans are mashed and fried; these are called *frijoles refritos* (refried beans), and they are usually served with breakfast or supper. Restaurants, however, now serve them at any meal.

The wide variety of *chiles* used in Mexican cooking is another distinguishing feature. These chiles are known by one name when they are fresh and another when dry. Drying can completely change the character of a chile: a *chile poblano* when fresh has a mild, tangy flavor, when dry (*chile ancho*) it has a pungent, rich, earthy taste. Some chiles are very hot and with little flavor (*chile de árbol, chile pequín, chile habanero*), others have a strong flavor and are not hot (*chile poblano, chile guajillo, chile cascabel*). One chile, the famous *jalapeño* (when smoked, it's called *chile chilpotle*), has a strong flavor and is very hot as well.

Meals

Breakfast (*el desayuno*) in Mexico can be either light or heavy. If eaten really early, it usually consists only of *café con leche* (coffee and milk) or hot chocolate and a piece of sweet bread. When eaten around nine or ten in the morning, it consists of a dish of eggs and tortillas cooked in a variety of ways, with fried beans, chile sauce, a plate of fruit, and coffee and juice. Mexican egg dishes include *huevos rancheros* – eggs that are poached or fried and served on a tortilla in a smoothly blended, spicy, tomato-based sauce. *Huevos a la mexicana* are eggs

> To ask for your check in a restaurant, say "*La cuenta, por favor.*"

scrambled with onion, tomato, and hot *chiles serranos*. *Chilaquiles* are tortillas that are dried or toasted and cooked in a red or green sauce with chicken and onion, and usually come with a little crumbled cheese and cream on top.

The **main meal** of the day in Mexico (*la comida*) is taken between 2 and 4pm, though this is giving way in the big cities to lighter and faster meals for workers. (The afternoon siesta, which traditionally follows, has also been a casualty of the same forces.) The comida usually begins with an appetizer or salad, and then a soup or rice dish, known as *la sopa*. Mexicans make very good soups that rarely disappoint. Afterwards comes the main course, or *plato fuerte*, a meat or fish dish, and then dessert and coffee. The most common dessert is flan, which is an egg custard much like the French *crème caramel* only with more body, and is often flavored with coconut or rum.

Supper (*la cena*) is taken around 8 o'clock or later. It is most often a small meal featuring some form of *antojitos*, which literally translated, means "little cravings." These dishes include *tacos*, simple *enchiladas*, *tortas*, *tostadas*, *chalupas*, *gorditas*, and a variety of others depending on where you are in Mexico. *Antojitos* usually are a big hit with visitors to Mexico who often want something to eat that's faster than a full meal.

It is quite common for Mexicans to have **snacks** in the late morning or late afternoon. Common snack foods are some of the above-mentioned *antojitos*, especially *tacos*. A taco is anything wrapped in a tortilla. The tortilla is usually soft, but it can also be fried. Most tacos have some sort of meat in them and are topped with chopped onion and cilantro (fresh coriander leaves) with sauces on the side. Most commonly found is the *taco al pastor*, which is pork marinated in the intensely red sauce of ground *achiote* seed (annatto), sour orange, and pineapple. Another great snack is the *licuado*, which is any fruit blended with ice and either water or milk. These are quite satisfying. Mexico is rich in a variety of tropical fruits, including mango, mamey, guayaba, zapote, papaya, chirimoya, and guanábana, as well as the more familiar coconut, banana, and orange.

Restaurants

Mexico has such a wonderful climate that it's no wonder that Mexicans enjoy eating outdoors. The many open-air restaurants in Mexico are often in the courtyards of colonial mansions or former convents, or under the stone archways that surround a plaza.

Whether indoors of outdoors, restaurants that cater to office workers and businesspeople tend to have, in addition to the regular menu items, a fixed-price, multi-course daily special for the large afternoon meal. This is called either a *comida corrida* or *menú del día*. It's your best bet for an inexpensive full meal.

Dishes that you might see on a restaurant menu include *mole*, of which there is a wide variety. The best known is *mole poblano*, a

This is the life! Sip an unhurried Mexican beer on the beach with just the birds for company.

dark brown, rich sauce made of ground *chiles*, toasted tortillas, bitter chocolate, and several spices, served over chicken or turkey and sprinkled with sesame seeds. Also, there is *pipián verde*, a sauce made of ground pumpkin seeds among other ingredients; it is served on poultry as well. Another classic is *puerco en adobado*, in which pork is marinated in a rich sauce made with two to three varieties of dried *chiles* and then cooked slowly. Fish dishes in Mexico are outstanding, and include *huachinango a la veracruzana*, red snapper in tomato sauce with olives, capers, and onions, *pescado al cilantro*, any fish in a tangy green sauce of husk tomatoes and cilantro, or *al mojo de ajo*, fish sautéed with little pieces of garlic. If you enjoy meat dishes that are slightly sweet, and you feel like splurging on calories, order a *chile en nogada* (providing it's in season). This is one of the most Baroque of Mexican dishes – a *chile poblano* stuffed

Maguey Spirits

Chances are that you'll be introduced to tequila before you even check into your hotel. Hostesses with pitchers of margaritas circulate in airports and hotel lobbies to welcome the thirsty tourists and hook them on Mexico's national tipple. It is deceptively mild and refreshing, but packs a wicked punch.

Tequila is made by fermenting juice extracted from the heart of the blue maguey plant. This is not a cactus, but an agave, a relative of the century plant. A cluster of thick leaves a couple of meters long rise from the ground around a tall spike that flowers at the top. In the center of the flower, like the heart of an artichoke, is the pineapple-shaped core, the piña, which is cut out, roasted, and squeezed to extract juice which, when fermented and aged, becomes tequila. True tequila, the real stuff, is limited by government regulation to liquor produced in the provinces around Guadalajara.

Mezcal is a specialty of the Oaxaca and certain regions of central Mexico. It is made from the juice of other maguey plants but in much the same manner. Mezcal has a stronger smell and taste. In Oaxaca, it is bottled with a maguey worm (gusano) pickled in booze. Both tequila and mezcal are around 76 proof. When aged, these liquors may be labeled añejo or viejo, and will have a golden color.

They are often taken neat in a shot glass after licking some salt off your fist. There's a ritual that goes along with it: raise the glass and say "arriba," lower it saying "abajo," bring it up to your chest with "al centro," and down it in one gulp after finishing with "adentro." ("Up, down, to the middle, and inside.") "Salud!" (To your health!) is good enough thereafter.

Pulque is the traditional drink of the peasant in central Mexico. It is the fermented juice of a couple of species of agave, and is slightly thick, white, and sweetish, and should be consumed as fresh as possible.

It's hangover time! Spring breakers are welcomed to Cancún with the promise of wild, intoxicating tequila fun in the sun!

with a mixture of ground chicken, pork, raisins, and almonds that is covered in a walnut cream sauce (in which the walnuts have had the thin brown skin removed so there is no bitterness) and sprinkled with pomegranate seeds.

To accompany your meal, there is a wide variety of Mexican beers. Coffee is most often served American style, but you can get it prepared in the traditional fashion of *café de olla* (cooked in an earthenware pot and spiced with cinnamon, cloves, and raw brown sugar) or as espresso. Tequila, of course, is the national tipple. A final thing to know about dining out in Mexico is that waiters will not want to appear unwelcoming and so will not bring the check

The Mexican staple, the ubiquitous tortilla, can be paired with almost anything for a delicious treat.

until you've asked for it, and even then, will not bring it very quickly. If you're pressed for time, ask for your check in advance. So enjoy yourself, and as Mexicans say when seeing others eat, "*¡Buen provecho!*" (may it do you good).

To Help You Order...

Here are a few terms that may enhance your dining experiences. Be bold and try to scrape by in Spanish – your efforts will be appreciated.

Do you have a table for one/ two/three/four people?	**¿ Tiene una mesa para una/ dos/tres/cuatro persona/personas?**
Do you have a menu?	**¿Tiene un menú?**
The bill, please.	**La cuenta, por favor.**

...And Read the Menu

aguacate avocado

ajo garlic

albahaca basil

alcachofas artichokes

ate fruit paste usually made of guava or quince

atole sweet drink made with corn dough

bistek steak

café coffee

café con leche strong black coffee served with steamed milk

calamares squid

camarones shrimp

carne tampiqueña thin cut of beef served grilled, with rice, an enchilada, rajas, and refried beans

cebolla onions

cerdo/puerco pork

cerveza beer

chilaquiles corn tortillas cooked in a sauce of chile peppers

chorizo spicy pork sausage

consomé clear broth

enchiladas tortillas covered in mole, tomato, or green sauce, filled with chicken or cheese, topped with cream, grated cheese, and chopped onions

ensalada salad

flan sweet custard made with eggs, milk, and vanilla

frijoles beans

horchata water flavored with rice and almonds

huevos eggs

mantequilla butter

mariscos seafood

mejillones mussels

mole spicy sauce with 30+ ingredients including chocolate

nopales cactus leaves often served diced as a salad with chopped tomatoes, onion, cilantro, and green chile

pan bread

pan dulce sweet rolls/pastries

papas potatoes

pescado fish

pollo chicken

pozole stew made with hominy and pork and/or chicken

quesadilla corn or flour tortilla folded in half filled with cheese, other fillings

queso cheese

rajas poblano peppers cut into strips, cooked with cream and cheese; sometimes with tomatoes and onions in the mixture

res beef

A dining experience is especially memorable with the Three Amigos for accompaniment.

salsa mexicana hot sauce made with chopped tomatoes, onions, green chile peppers, and cilantro

salsa roja hot sauce made with red chile peppers and tomato

salsa verde sauce made with green peppers and green tomatoes

sopa soup

sopa de lima chicken broth flavored with lime wedges, served with pieces of chicken

taco corn or flour tortilla stuffed with any number of fillings

tamal corn batter stuffed with sweet or savory fillings, wrapped in corn husks, and steamed

HANDY TRAVEL TIPS

An A–Z Summary of Practical Information

A

ACCOMMODATION (*alojamiento*) (See also Camping)

Prices don't always tell the whole story of what to expect from a hotel in Mexico. A charming hotel in an old mansion may charge lower rates simply because it doesn't have TVs or a pool, while run-of-the-mill hostelries that feature such amenities may cost twice as much. Also, depending on the various package deals available and seasonal discounts, the same lodging may go for very different prices. As a rule, rates at the beaches and other resorts are higher from mid-December until Easter. In most cases you'll need to reserve in advance during this popular period. Any time of year, travelers arriving without reservations will find hotel information desks and phones in the major airports. The most economical accommodations can usually be found in small hotels near the central part of the city, or around the zócalo, and in the older parts of a town. If you plan to spend a few weeks in Mexico at one place, you may want to rent an apartment; try looking in the local newspapers or call the local tourist information office, which can usually direct you to the most reliable places.

I'd like a single/double room with bath/shower.	**Quisiera una habitación sencilla/doble con baño/regadera**.
What's the rate per night?	**¿Cuál es la tarifa por noche?**
Where is there a cheap hotel?	**¿Dónde hay un hotel económico?**

AIRPORTS

Benito Juárez International Airport in Mexico City is actually inside the city limits. Seven national and 16 international airlines use the facilities, which may appear to be a great buzzing confusion at first, but are quite easy to navigate. Follow the signs to your luggage pickup point (*entrega de equipajes*), which will be area E for international flights and A for most national arrivals. When arriving on an international flight, you will clear immigration, which is on the same level as the arrival gates, and then go downstairs to claim your luggage. In the international arrival area, you may use one of the carts that are available at no charge in the baggage claim area to take your luggage to the customs clearance area, but not beyond; once you exit, porters will be waiting to help you to your taxi. Tip about 10 pesos per bag. Clearance through customs is fairly quick.

In the long hall outside the luggage areas, you will find banks and *casas de cambio* (private moneychangers, who give almost the same rate as a bank), where you can buy and sell your dollars and pesos. There are souvenir shops, bookstores and newsstands, places to eat and drink, hotel and travel information services, a post office (near Area A), one hotel inside the terminal and another linked to the terminal by a walkway, luggage lockers (*depósito de equipajes*), and many other useful services. If you need help, go to one of the information booths.

In more or less all cities of Mexico, yellow and white (mostly white) vehicles marked *transportación terrestre* are pre-paid inside the airport or just outside on the sidewalk. (Pay no attention to people calling "Taxi!" or to anyone offering guide services.) When you get to the head of the line tell the dispatcher your destination, which he will relay to the cab driver. Give your pre-paid ticket to the driver, then sit back and relax.

There is a US$12 airport departure tax; most airlines include this tax in the price of your ticket, but double-check to make sure you are not caught by surprise at the airport upon leaving.

| Porter! | **¡Maletero!** |
| Where's the bus for…? | **¿Dónde se toma el camión para…?** |

B

BARGAINING

Street and market vendors are prepared to bargain. As a rule of thumb, you should start by offering about 20 percent less than you are willing to pay. However you shouldn't enter into the haggling game unless really ready to buy, and never propose a price that is insultingly low. You can always break off a deadlock in a pleasant way, saying "*gracias,*" and indicating that you want to look around. When you come back, you'll probably be able to knock at least 20 percent off the asking price without shedding blood. If haggling upsets you, simply ask if there is a discount (*¿Me hace una rebaja?*) Rest assured that whatever you finally pay, the seller is making a profit and you'll probably have your bargain.

How much is that?   **¿Cuánto es?**

BUDGETING FOR YOUR TRIP

Value is the operative word when traveling to Mexico, and is among the country's principal appeals. You can find great bargains anywhere in Mexico, especially in colonial cities, coastal villages, and smaller towns, but in Mexico City and well-developed resort areas as well. While you can encounter hotels that charge more than 1,500 pesos per night, budget conscious travelers can find clean and comfortable accommodations ranging between 250 and 400 pesos per room per night. These rooms are usually for two persons, and it is very common for children to be able to stay for free in their parent's room. Dining is an excellent value when compared to most US or European destinations, with *comidas corridas* (a fixed-price lunch) costing between 25 and 35 pesos for a full meal with soup, rice or pasta, a main course, dessert, fruit flavored water, coffee, and bread or *tortillas*. Breakfast and dinner can be just as inexpensive. Travel is also inexpensive, with intra-city bus rides rarely costing more than 5 pesos and a long, 1,200-km (720-mile) trip costing around 700 pesos.

C

CAMPING

There are campsites throughout the country, including two sites in the vicinity of Mexico City itself. Most of the organized campgrounds are found in the northern states and along the Pacific Coast, down to the state of Jalisco. Some hotels have places for camping as well. While it is usually safe to camp on most beaches, it is a good idea to take as many precautions as possible (ask locals about any regulations and safety). For information about camping in Mexico and a complete list of camping grounds and trailer parks in Mexico, contact INFOTUR: Presidente Mazaryk 172, Col. Polanco, México, D.F., C.P. 11587; Tel. 800-903-9200 or (55) 5250-0123.

May we camp here?	**¿Podemos acampar aquí?**
We have a tent/trailer.	**Tenemos una tienda de campaña/ un trailer.**

CAR RENTAL/HIRE (*Arrendamiento de automóviles*)
(See also DRIVING)

All well-known international companies and many reliable national ones rent to adults with a valid driver's license and a credit card. Shop around for the best deal, but keep in mind that rental cars are not a bargain in Mexico, because cars and their upkeep in general are more expensive here than they are elsewhere. Rates vary, but you can expect to pay 350 to 750 pesos per day with unlimited mileage; it is advisable to take the insurance included option.

I'd like to rent a car	**Quisiera rentar un coche**
for today/tomorrow.	**Para hoy/mañana.**
for one day/one week.	**Por un día/una semana.**

CLIMATE

Mexico is a vast country with varied topography and a great variety of climates within its territory. Coastal regions enjoy summer-like, almost tropical weather practically year round, with temperatures ranging between 22° and 32°C (72° and 90°F), with rainy seasons usually running between June and November. Winter mornings and evenings can be cool, especially along the Baja coast and most northern beach destinations. Mexico City and other inland colonial cities are cool in the winter, with temperatures occasionally dropping below 10°C (50°F), and pleasantly warm during spring and summer, with temperatures reaching the mid 20s C (70s F); however, evenings and mornings are almost always cool.

CLOTHING

The lightest and most informal summer clothing is fine for all the beach resorts year round, but you should bring a light sweater and windbreaker for the occasional cool mornings and evenings; also keep in mind that at high altitudes and in the desert, winter temperatures can dip quite low. A raincoat or umbrella will come in handy from May to October. Ties and jackets for men are virtually unknown at beach resorts but are commonly worn in the better restaurants of the big cities, particularly in the evening. Don't wear extra-short miniskirts or shorts (the latter goes for men as well) anywhere in Mexico apart from the big tourist resorts. As a general rule, in the more remote the villages both men and women should take care to dress conservatively. Sandals as well as a comfortable pair of walking shoes (for scrambling over ruins and pyramids) are a must.

COMPLAINTS (*reclamación*)

If you have a complaint against a hotel, restaurant, taxi driver, or tourist guide, and you can't work it out on the spot, go to the Procuraduría Federal del Consumidor (Profeco). In Mexico City the number is (55) 5578-7795. There is a local Profeco office in all major destinations within in Mexico. For grievances involving people or organizations not normally associated with the tourism industry, it is recommended that you go to the local police station. In Mexico City go to the Procuraduría del Turista on Florencia #20; Tel. (55) 5625-8153.

COURTESIES AND SOCIAL CUSTOMS

Mexicans are by nature and upbringing dignified and courteous. Passengers leaving a bus may say "*gracias*" (thank you) to the bus driver and receive a "*para servirle*" (at your service) in reply. If you sneeze, someone will be sure to say "*salud*," to which you reply "*gracias*." Always address any stranger as *Señor, Joven* (young man), or *Señorita* (even older women, unless you know they are married). Liberally use *gracias, por favor* (please), and *muy amable* (very kind of you). Shaking hands upon meeting and leaving is expected. Don't be surprised if the handshake is a double-action grip involving locking thumbs. Male friends often greet each other with a bear hug and back-slapping, called an *abrazo*; women will kiss each other on the cheek, and it is also common for men and women to kiss on the cheek when greeting and saying good-bye – even in business situations. Female friends may walk arm-in-arm down the street.

Be aware that a Mexican's desire to please and avoid the negative may lead to waiters not bringing the bill until requested, clerks not volunteering that the office will be closed the next day due to a holiday, strangers giving directions to places they've never heard of, and people agreeing to things they'll never carry out and accepting invitations they won't honor. Students of these matters say that the ancient Indian belief that only the gods decide destiny survives today in an attitude of futility concerning definite plans. There may be something to this. The *mañana* stereotype, though, bears no resemblance whatsoever to the hard working artisans, farmers, and factory and office workers who turn the wheels of modern Mexico.

Women should keep in mind that there is a prevalent attitude that foreign women, especially those travelling alone, are promiscuous and sexually available. The only way around eventual misunderstandings is to dress and behave conservatively, and not to respond in any way to various attentions and provocations. Women shouldn't have any trouble being served in hotels or regular bars and restaurants, but they are not admitted into local *cantinas* or *pulquerías*. In fact, in certain places even foreign men won't be allowed into the *pulquerías*. It is not an insult but just that certain social and cultural practices are still private and Mexicans intend to keep it that way.

CRIME AND SAFETY

Pickpockets operate wherever there are crowds; be alert. There is a brisk trade in US passports; never leave yours in the hotel room. Use the hotel safe for valuables and use the chain lock on your hotel room. Always lock your car, and don't leave valuables in sight. Don't leave luggage or packages unattended. If you wear a fanny-pack make sure that the pouch is always facing to the front. Women should avoid purses with large openings that do not zip or have a flap that can be secured. Taxis have been involved in several crimes in Mexico City; use only taxis arranged through a hotel or an official agency. ATMs are also trouble spots – never use one unless other people are around and you feel safe in their presence. The Procuraduría del Turista was created to help tourists that are victims of a crime. To contact them call (55) 5625-8153, (55) 5625-8154, or (55) 5625-8763 in Mexico City. Elsewhere in Mexico, dial 060 or 080 to report a crime.

I want to report a theft.　　　　**Quiero denunciar(reportar) un robo.**

CUSTOMS AND ENTRY REQUIREMENTS

Formalities at a border or airport are quick and simple. Instead of a visa, visitors must have a **tourist card,** obtainable upon proof of citizenship from airlines serving Mexico and at border points. This free card is valid for three months and is renewable for another three, though the renewal process is somewhat time-consuming. The tourist card will be stamped upon entry and it must be kept with you for presentation on departure. Keep your card in a safe place with your passport and other documents – if you lose it, file a report at the local tourist office to avoid delays on departure. Tourists may visit Mexico for 72 hours without a tourist card and without paying the US$15 internment tax if they enter at the US-Mexico border and stay within a specified zone.

The following chart shows what duty-free items you may take into Mexico and, when returning home, to your own country:

	Cigarettes		Cigars		Tobacco	Spirit		Wine
Mexico	500	or	100	or	250g	3l		
Australia	250	or	200	or	250g	1.1l	or	1.1l
Canada	200	or	50	and	1 kg	1.1l	or	1.1l
Ireland	200	or	50	or	250g	1l	or	2l
N. Zealand	200	or	50	or	250g	1.1l	and	4.5l
S. Africa	400	and	50	and	250g	1l	and	2l

UK	200	or	50	or	250g	1*l*	and	2*l*
US	200	and	50	and	*	1*l*	and	1*l*

*A reasonable quantity

Currency restrictions. Non-residents may import or export any amount of freely convertible foreign currency into Mexico provided it is declared upon arrival. There is also no limit to the amount of Mexican currency you may carry into or out of Mexico.

I have nothing to declare.   **No tengo nada que declarar.**

 D

DRIVING

Any valid driver's license is accepted in Mexico. To rent a car the driver must be at least 21 years of age. If you bring your own car, you must present proof of ownership at the border, where it will be registered with your tourist card. Only the owner of the car can drive it; otherwise, you need to have a notarized letter stating the names of those who will be driving. Take out full accident and liability Mexican insurance at the border, since coverage from most other countries does not apply. Have your car thoroughly checked before departure and bring along any spare parts such as a fan belt and oil filter, which may be difficult to obtain. A container of water and a gas-can are good insurance. Get a good road map from your automobile club (they are not sold in gas stations); it should also describe the common road signs.

Most Mexican surfaced roads are two-lane, very winding in the mountains and often without shoulders. While the main highways are generally in good condition, be careful of rounding curves and topping rises: there may be cows or a poorly marked hazard just out of sight; it is not uncommon to encounter a bus slowly passing an even slower vehicle. Try to avoid driving at night – traffic with no headlights abound. Rocks or branches on the road are often placed there to indicate a broken down vehicle ahead or a huge pothole in the middle of the road. Look out for sign in villages and near schools announcing *topes* or *vibradores*. These

Mexico

humps are placed across the road to slow traffic and are nasty to hit at high speed. Sometimes they are hard to spot and seem to blend in with the rest of the road, so keep your eyes open. Visitors are strongly advised to avoid driving in Mexico City if they can.

If you have car trouble, raise your hood and wait for the "Green Angels" (*Ángeles Verdes*). These green government repair trucks patrol the main routes from 8am–7pm, making minor repairs and supplying emergency gasoline, charging only the cost of the materials. If you have a cellphone, you can call them at (55) 5250-8221. An alternative is to flag a passing car or truck and ask the driver to alert the Green Angels on your behalf, keeping in mind that most truck operators don't speak English.

Pemex is the federal gasoline supplier, and while gasoline is still distributed through the government only, some gas stations are now independent concessions. The new ones usually include well-stocked convenience stores and restrooms that are reasonably clean. There are two kinds of gasoline, both unleaded: *magna,* with an 83 octane, and *premium,* with 97 octane. Diesel fuel is available, but not all gas stations carry it. It is recommended to use a gas additive, such as STP or Bardahl – especially if you are driving a vehicle with fuel-injection, because octane ratings are not the same as in the US and sometimes slow the combustion. Fill up whenever your tank is half-empty: it may be a long drive to the next station. Tip gas station attendants for filling the tank and other services, such as cleaning the windshield. Credit cards are not accepted at most gas stations.

Fluid measures

Distance

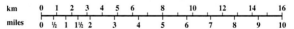

Most Mexican road signs are the standard international pictographs. But you may encounter these written signs:

Aduana	Customs
Alto	Stop
Autopista (de cuota)	(Toll) highway
Camino deteriorado (en malas condiciones)	Bad road
Ceda el paso	Yield
Cruce peligroso	Dangerous crossing
Cuidado	Caution
Despacio	Slow
Desviación	Detour
Escuela	School
Peligro	Danger
Prohibido estacionarse	No parking
Prohibido (No) rebasar	No passing
Puesto de socorro	First-aid station
Puente angosto	Narrow bridge
Salida de camiones	Truck exit
(International) driver's license	**Licencia para manejar (internacional)**
Car registration papers	**Registro del automóvil**
Are we on the right road for…?	**¿Es esta la carretera hacia…?**
Fill the tank, top grade, please.	**Llénelo, con premium, por favor.**
Check the oil/tires/battery.	**Revise el aceite/las llantas/la batería.**
I've had a breakdown.	**Mi carro se ha descompuesto.**
There's been an accident.	**Ha habido un accidente.**

Mexico

DRUGS

Stay away from them. For all the talk about "Acapulco Gold," drugs are illegal and not tolerated in Mexico. If the Federal Police pick you up on suspicion of drug possession or dealing, you can be held for an extended period of time without trial – in Mexico, the underlying principle of the law is that you are assumed guilty until proven innocent. If you are charged with even possession, a jail sentence is inevitable.

ELECTRICITY

Mexico is on the US and Canadian system of 120 volts, 60 cycles; outlets, however, are equipped for two flat pins only. Appliances using other systems will require a transformer and/or an adapter plug (if you have three-prong appliances, you'll find a three-prong to two-prong adapter especially handy). Voltage variations are very common, so it is recommended to have a surge protector and regulator.

EMBASSIES AND CONSULATES

Embassies

Australia: Ruben Dario 55, Col. Polanco, Mexico City, CP 11580; Tel. (55) 5531-5225

Canada: Schiller 529, Colonia Polanco, Mexico City, CP 11570; Tel. (55) 5724-7900

New Zealand: José Luis LaGrange 103, 10th floor, Col. Polanco, Mexico City, CP 11570; Tel. (55) 5283-9460

South Africa: Andres Bello 10, 9th floor, Col. Polanco, Mexico City, CP 11510; Tel (55) 5282-9260

UK: Rio Lerma 71, Col. Cuauhtemoc, Mexico City, CP 06500; Tel. (55) 5207-2089

US: Paseo de la Reforma 305, Col. Cuauhtemoc, Mexico City, CP 06500; Tel. (55) 5209-9100

Consulates

Canada: Hotel Fiesta Americana L-31, Guadalajara, Jalisco CP 44100; Tel. (33) 3615-6215

Centro Comercial Marbella, Local 23, Prolongación Farallón S/N, Acapulco, Guerrero CP 39670; Tel. (744) 484-1305

Germán Gedovious 10411–101, Condominio del Parque, Zona Río, Tijuana, CP 22320, BCN; Tel. (664) 684-0461

Hotel Playa Mazatlán, Rodolfo T. Loaiza 202, Zona Dorada, Mazatlán, CP 82110, Sinaloa; Tel. (623) 684-0461

Plaza José Green, Local 9, Blvd, Mijares s/n, San José del Cabo, CP 23400, BCS; Tel. (624) 142-4333

Pino Suarez 700, Local 11B, Multiplaza Brena, Oaxaca, CP 68000. Oaxaca; Tel. (951) 513-3777

Plaza Caracol II, 3rd floor, local 330, Blvd, Kukulkan Km 8.5, Cancún, CP 77500, Quintana Roo; Tel. (998) 883-3360

Zaragoza #160, Interior 10, Col. Centro, Puerto Vallarta, CP 48300, Jalisco; Tel. (322) 222-5398

Edificio Kalos, Piso C-1, Local 108-A, Zaragoza 1300 Sur and Constitución, Monterrey, CP 06400, Nuevo León; Tel. (81) 8344-2753

UK: Centro Internacional Acapulco, Costera Miguel Alemán, Acapulco, Guerrero, CP 39851; Tel. (744) 484-1735

Royal Sands, Blvd, Kukulcán Km 13.5, Cancún, Quintana Roo, CP 77500; Tel. (998) 881-0100

Fresno 185, Campestre Juárez, Cd. Juárez, Chihuahua, CP 32460; Tel. (614) 617-5791

Mexico

Paseo del Edén 2449-4, Prolongación Colinas de San Javier, Guadalajara, Jalisco CP 45110; Tel. (33) 3343-2296

Calle 58 # 450 X 53, Merida, Yucatán, CP 97000; Tel. (999) 928-6152

Ave. Ricardo Margáin Zozaya 240, 2nd Floor, Monterrey, Nuevo León, CP 66200; Tel. (81) 8356-5359

Independencia 1349-1, Veracruz, Veracruz, CP 91700; Tel. (224) 932-7399

CEPROTUR, Plaza Santo Domingo Int 13, Alcalá and Allende, Oaxaca, Oaxaca, CP 68000; Tel. (951) 516-7280

US: Progreso 175, Guadalajara, Jalisco, CP 44100; Tel. (33) 3825-2700

Monterrey 141 Pte., Hermosillo, Sonora, CP 83260; Tel. (662) 217-2375

Ave. Primera 2002 and Azaleas, Matamoros, Tamaulipas, CP 87330; Tel. (868) 812-4402

Paseo Montejo 453, Merida, Yucatán, CP 97000; Tel. (999) 925-5011

Tapachula 96, Col. Hipódromo, Tijuana, BCN, CP 22420; Tel. (664) 622-7400

Hotel Acapulco Continental, Office 14, Acapulco, Guerrero, CP 39580; Tel. (744) 469-0556

Blvd. Marina and Pedregal #1, Office 3, Cabo San Lucas, BCS; Tel. (624) 143-3566

Plaza Caracol II, 2nd floor, Local 320-323, Blvd. Kukulcán Km 8.5, Cancún, Quintana Roo, CP 77500; Tel. (998) 883-0272

Plaza Ambiente, Ixtapa, Zihutanejo, Guerrero, CP 40880; Tel. (755) 553-1108

Macedonio Alcalá 201, Office 206, Oaxaca, Oaxaca, CP 68000; Tel. (951) 514-3054

Vallarta Building, Zaragoza 160, 2nd floor, Puerto Vallarta, Jalisco, CP 48300; Tel. (322) 222-0069

Venustiano Carranza 2076–41, San Luis Potosí, SLP, CP 96000; Tel. (444) 812-7802

Dr. Hernándeaz Macías 72, San Miguel de Allende, Guanajuato, CP 37700; Tel. (415) 152-2357

G

GETTING THERE

Most international flights arrive in Mexico City airport. International airlines have direct flights into Mexico from almost every major airport in the US, with the most flights arriving from New York, Chicago, Los Angeles, Dallas, Houston, and Miami. Overseas airports with direct flights to Mexico include Frankfurt, London, Paris, Amsterdam, Madrid, Sydney, and Johannesburg (most of these flights operate weekly or several times a week); in many cases, European travelers to Mexico may find it more convenient to make connections in New York or another US gateway. During the high season (winter months) several airlines fly directly form US and overseas airports into resort areas like Cancún, Puerto Vallarta, and Los Cabos.

GUIDES

All types of ingratiating types will offer to be helpful. If you want a guide, get one who is accredited by the Secretariat of Tourism through your hotel or a travel agency. At major museums and archaeological sites, tours by official guides are available. The more foreign tourists that visit a place, the more likely it is that you can find guides who speak foreign languages. It is customary to give tour guides a tip.

We'd like an English speaking guide.	**Queremos un guía que hable inglés.**
I need an English interpreter.	**Necesito un intérprete en inglés.**

H

HEALTH AND MEDICAL CARE

No vaccinations are required for entry, but your doctor may recommend updating your tetanus and polio immunization and suggest a vaccination as a hepatitis deterrent. Mexico City and many other towns are above 1,335 m (7,000 ft), an altitude that will affect some visitors more than others. If you notice shortness of breath, a slight headache, and a tired feeling, take it easy on exercise, food, and drink for the first day or two and the symptoms will disappear. Along with the altitude, in Mexico City the pollution will probably also affect the way you feel – breathing the air on an average day is said to be the equivalent to smoking two packs of cigarettes (see page 42).

The most notorious Mexican health hazard, variously known to tourists as the *turista* or "Moctezuma's Revenge," is a relatively harmless combination of diarrhea and upset stomach that travelers encounter worldwide. It is caused mostly by the different chemicals and bacteria encountered in the water. The best way to avoid this nuisance is to refrain from drinking tap water, consume purified bottled water, and take ice only in places where you are quite sure that it is made from purified water, such as in restaurants that cater to tourists. The machine-made ice cubes in first class establishments are usually safe, but "usually" doesn't mean "always" – you can always ask for drinks *sin hielo* (without ice). It is hard to pass up the delicious fruits and juices in markets or the savory snacks offered at street stands, but it is best to play it safe until you've been in the country for a couple of weeks and have made peace with the unfamiliar local bacteria.

a bottle of mineral water	**una botella de agua mineral**
carbonated/non-carbonated	**con gas/sin gas**

If you do succumb, take plenty of liquids, such as herbal tea like *manzanilla* (chamomille) with a little salt (a pinch) and sugar (a teaspoon), or sports drinks like Gatorade that will replenish some of the minerals you loose. Mexican pharmacies sell most drugs without prescription and are familiar with proven local remedies for *turista*. In almost every tourist destination there are pharmacies that open 24 hours a day and even deliver without an extra charge. Otherwise, there are pharmacies that remain "on duty" after hours, on weekends, and holidays. Any pharmacy in town will tell you the location of the "*farmacia de turno.*"

In an emergency, most first class hotels have a doctor on call who will speak English and other foreign languages. Embassies also have a list of multi-lingual doctors. A couple of hospitals with bilingual staff are: American-British Cowdray (ABC) Hospital, Calle Sur 132 136, Colonia Las Américas, Mexico City; Tel. (55) 5230-8000, and Mexico-Americano Hospital, Colomos 2110, Guadalajara, Jalisco; Tel. (33) 3642-7152.

Get me a doctor, quickly!	**¡Llamen a un médico, rápido!**

HOLIDAYS *(día festivo)*

The Mexican fiesta calendar offers a full array of celebrations to choose from. There are states that seem to have a celebration, religious, political, or otherwise, almost every day of the year. The official holidays are:

1 January	*Año Nuevo*	New Year's Day
5 February	*Aniversario de la Constitución*	Constitution Day
21 March	*Nacimiento de Benito Juárez*	Benito Juárez's Birthday
1 May	*Día del Trabajo*	Labor Day
5 May	*Batalla de Puebla*	Anniversary of the Battle of Puebla
1 September	*Informe presidencial*	First day of Congress
16 September	*Día de la Independencia*	Independence Day

Mexico

12 October	*Dia de la Raza*	Columbus Day, "Day of the Race"
2 November	*Dia de los Muertos*	All Souls' Day
20 November	*Aniversario de la Revolucion*	Anniversary of the Revolution
12 December	*Nuestra Señora de Guadalupe*	Our Lady of Guadalupe
25 December	*Navidad*	Christmas Day
Movable dates	*Pascua, Semana Santa*	Easter, Holy Week

Are you open tomorrow?   **¿Está abierto mañana?**

L

LANGUAGE

Mexico is the largest Spanish-speaking country in the world. In addition, Mexican Indians speak 58 indigenous languages or dialects, with Spanish as their *lingua franca*. English is understood in hotels and tourists oriented establishments throughout the country – even Indian women in the market may be able to quote prices in English. Official guides qualified in foreign languages may be engaged through travel agencies or located through local tourism offices. But any Spanish you possess or phrases you learn will be appreciated by Mexicans and will make asking directions, shopping, and ordering food easier. Remember – you are a visitor in this country and locals serve you a courtesy by speaking, or trying to speak, your language. The least you can try to do is return the courtesy by trying to speak some phrases in Spanish, or at least not get frustrated if somebody doesn't speak English.

Numbers

0	**cero**	4	**cuatro**
1	**uno**	5	**cinco**
2	**dos**	6	**seis**
3	**tres**	7	**siete**

8	ocho	21	veintiuno
9	nueve	30	treinta
10	diez	40	cuarenta
11	once	50	cincuenta
12	doce	60	sesenta
13	trece	70	setenta
14	catorce	80	ochenta
15	quince	90	noventa
16	dieciséis	100	cien
17	diecisiete	101	ciento uno
18	dieciocho	500	quinientos
19	diecinueve	1,000	mil
20	veinte		

Days

Sunday	domingo
Monday	lunes
Tuesday	martes
Wednesday	miércoles
Thursday	jueves
Friday	viernes
Saturday	sábado

Months

January	enero
February	febrero
March	marzo
April	abril
May	mayo
June	junio

Mexico

July	**julio**
August	**agosto**
September	**septiembre**
October	**octubre**
November	**noviembre**
December	**diciembre**

Some useful expressions

Yes/no	**si/no**
Please/thank you	**por favor/gracias**
Excuse me/you're welcome	**perdón/de nada**
Where/when/how	**dónde/cuándo/cómo**
How long/how far	**cuánto tiempo/qué distancia**
Yesterday/today/tomorrow	**ayer/hoy/mañana**
Day/week/month/year	**día/semana/mes/año**
Left/right	**izquierda/derecha**
Up/down	**arriba/abajo**
Good/bad	**bueno/malo**
Big/small	**grande/pequeño**
Cheap/expensive	**barato/caro**
Hot/cold	**caliente/frio**
Old/new	**viejo/nuevo**
Open/closed	**abierto/cerrado**
Do you speak English?	**¿Habla inglés?**
I don't understand	**No entiendo**
Please write it down	**Escríbalo, por favor**
Help me please	**Ayúdeme, por favor**
I'd like...	**Quisiera...**
What time is it?	**¿Qué hora es?**

LOST PROPERTY

Every state and major city of Mexico has a Tourist Department with a telephone number for tourist assistance (see TOURIST INFORMATION). If your hotel can't solve your problem, ask someone to contact this number or the local Policia Judicial for you.

Lost children will normally be delivered to the neighborhood police station, which is where you should go if your child gets lost – or if you find a lost child. The Procuraduría Federal de la Nación offers a nation wide service to locate lost people and property. To make a report or an inquiry contact them at Tel. (55) 5242-6235 or (55) 5242-6233. Locatel in Mexico City offers a computerized telephone service, (5) 658-1111, that provides information about lost persons and stolen vehicles. Whenever there is an incident where property is lost or stolen, you must report it to the local office of the Procuraduría – in Mexico City call the Procuraduría del Turista, Tel. (55) 5625-8153; it is especially important to report a lost passport or other personal documents.

I've lost my wallet/	**He perdido mi cartera/**
purse/passport	**bolsa/pasaporte.**

MEDIA

A considerable number of daily newspapers are published in Mexico City, most of them heavily oriented toward local and national events. One English-language daily, *The News*, is distributed where tourists are found. Only in the leading hotels and bookstores of the main cities will you find foreign newspapers. Foreign magazines are easier to find, since they are usually available in drugstores and tobacco shops at hotels and airports. While you can occasionally find European and even a few Asian publications, it is more common to find US newspapers and magazines. For those who are interested in staying up to date with the international news, sometimes it is easier to do through television, since most hotels offer either cable or satellite TV with at least one US channel that broadcasts current news. There are several radio stations that play music in Spanish and English all day. StereoRey is a FM station with broadcasting antennas in most of Mexico.

| Have you any magazines/ newspapers in English? | **¿Tiene revistas/ periódicos en inglés?** |

MEETING PEOPLE

Mexicans are exceptionally friendly people, though you must first overcome their initial reserve. This can be accomplished swiftly by a smile and a question or remark in Spanish. If someone recognizes your accent and can speak your language they will be delighted to demonstrate it.

Mexican women follow rigid codes of behavior and may not respond if they misinterpret your interest. On the other hand, men who approach you, usually on the street and often asking "Where are you from?," are most likely hustlers. When you are out for a night in the town, it is important to remember that while Mexican men are friendly and love to have fun, they are also very jealous of their girlfriends, sisters, and any other female acquaintance that may be part of the group. So it is important to act in a polite and courteous manner.

MONEY

The currency of Mexico is the **peso**, designated by the international sign for currency $ (in this book we have not used the $ sign for the peso, to avoid confusion with the US$). A peso is divided in 100 centavos, but you will only find 10, 20, and 50 centavo coins, and usually prices are rounded to the closest peso amount, so instead of something being 1.50 (one peso and fifty centavos) it will be 2 pesos. There are also coins worth 1, 5, 10 and 20 pesos. Bills are issued in 20, 50, 100, 200, and 500 pesos. The bills have different sizes and colors. Be careful not to accept bills that are torn, ripped, taped, or otherwise damaged, as neither businesses nor banks will accept them.

Banking hours are normally Monday–Friday 9am–3pm. Increasingly, banks are extending their hours until 5 or 7pm and some are now open on Saturday 10am–2pm. Most banks will exchange foreign currency during banking hours. Keep in mind that banks are usually crowded on the first, 15th, and last day of the month, because these are paydays for most employees. Fridays are especially busy days for all banks. Many banks now have **ATMs**, where you can withdraw funds from your bank account in pesos, and usually at a favorable exchange rate. However, be extremely cautious when using these machines, especially in Mexico City and other large cities. Try to use them in well-trafficked areas only during daylight hours.

Exchanging money. There is no black market and the peso fluctuates daily a tiny bit, a good reason for not cashing too much currency at one time. All banks offer the same rate as it is published daily in Mexico City and broadcast to all banks. Some banks charge a 1 percent fee to exchange travelers checks, and you will need your passport as an ID. **Private Exchange Houses** (Casas de Cambio) will exchange currency and travelers' checks at or near bank rates, and are open longer hours and on many holidays. Try to keep small change in pesos, such as 5 and 10 peso coins, for tipping, paying taxis, and small purchases. Merchants and drivers frequently can't (or won't) make change. Hotels will exchange money at all hours, but at less favorable rates.

Leading credit cards are widely accepted throughout Mexico, though not in most gas stations. If you are planning to charge a hotel bill or a meal, it is advisable to ask which credit cards are honored in the establishment. Most hotels, restaurants, and shops in resort areas will take travelers' checks. US dollars are widely accepted in resort areas, airports, and border towns, and sometimes the prices are even quoted in dollars.

I want to change	**Quiero cambiar**
some dollars/pounds.	**dólares/libras esterlinas.**

Do you accept traveler's checks?	**¿Acepta cheques de viajero?**

Can I pay with	**¿Puedo pagar con**
this credit card?	**esta tarjeta de crédito?**

Mexico

How much?	**¿Cuánto es?**
Have you anything cheaper?	**¿Tiene algo más barato?**

OPEN HOURS

In the capital and major cities, shops and offices open at 9 or 10am and remain open until 6pm or even later. In most resorts and in cities in the interior of Mexico, shops and offices usually close from 2 until 4 and then remain open until 7 or 8pm in the evening. Almost everywhere in the country museums are open from 10am until 6pm, and are usually closed on Mondays. Banks have traditionally been open 9am–3pm; however, more and more banks are modernizing, and in the process, extending their office hours until 5, 6 or 7pm. Some are also opening on Saturdays 10am–2pm. As a rule, the larger the city, the longer the business hours. Sunday is still the day-off par excellence in Mexico, when most offices and shops closed.

P

PHOTOGRAPHY

Well-known brands of film are widely available in all varieties. Processing can be done in an hour in most cities and resort areas, and there are overnight or two-day developing places all over Mexico. However, slides (*diapositives*) do take longer, up to a week, and only certain labs offer that service, so you are better off sticking to prints. Videocassettes are also in good supply; however, while pre-made videos are compatible with systems in the US, they will not run on many European systems. Remember that the sun is very bright in the coastal areas. You won't need high-speed film for most purposes, but the use of a flash is restricted in many artistic and archaeological sites. In quite a few museums, tourist sites, and churches you may have to check your camera at the entrance or pay a fee to use it. Also, remember that many people – especially in more remote areas – do not like to have their pictures taken and you must respect their wishes.

I'd like a film for this camera	**Quisiera un rollo para esta cámara**
a film for color pictures	**un rollo para fotografía en color**
for black and white	**en blanco y negro**
for color slides	**para transparencias**
35-mm-film	**de treinta y cinco milímetros**
super-8	**super ocho**
How long will it take to develop	**¿Cuánto tardará en revelar**
(and print) this film?	**(e imprimir) este rollo?**
May I take a picture?	**¿Puedo tomar una foto?**

POLICE

There are several branches of the police in Mexico. There are the local or municipal police – the ones who intervene in case of a mishap in any public area such as parks, restaurants, bars, etc. They also have a traffic division, in charge of all traffic related incidents. There are also the State, Federal, and Judicial police. Each one has different jurisdictions, but in case of an incident where the intervention of the police is needed, any passing patrol, regardless of their jurisdiction, will offer assistance. The Ministerio Público is the division in charge of crimes, and the office you need to report to in case of a robbery or assault. In Mexico City, you can call the bilingual staff at the Procuraduría del Turista; Tel. (55) 5625-8153 or (55) 5625-8154, in case of an incident that you need to report. Everywhere in Mexico, you can dial 060 or 080 for police assistance in case of an emergency, but operators are generally not bilingual.

POST OFFICES *(correos)*

Post offices are usually open Monday–Friday 9am–6pm and Saturday 9am–1pm.

Mexico

General delivery (*lista de correos*). If you don't know in advance where you'll be staying and you plan an extended stay in any one place, you can have your mail addressed to the *Lista de Correos* in any town. The office will hold the mail for ten days before returning it.

Mailboxes (*buzones*). If you have a choice of slots, always put international mail in the one marked *Aereo* (air mail); *Terrestre* is for surface mail.

Have you received any mail for…?	**¿Tiene correo para…?** or **¿Ha recibido correo para…?**
stamp / letter / postcard	**timbre / carta / tarjeta postal**
special delivery (express)	**urgente**
airmail	**correo aéreo**
registered	**correo certificado**

PUBLIC TRANSPORTATION

By air. Internal air travel is the most efficient way to travel around the country. Rates are relatively low and you'll avoid time-consuming and tiresome bus or train trips; even if you don't make arrangements before arriving in Mexico, you can check with any local travel agent for schedules and fares.

By bus. In town and between cities, the average Mexican prefers to travel by bus. Without a doubt the bus system is the cheapest most practical way to travel around town and around the country. For in-town service, routes usually run along the main streets. To travel between towns and cities, most travelers prefer the deluxe and first class buses. Tickets are usually sold at the bus terminal or through a local travel agent. The most accurate source of information about rates and schedule is the station itself. When planning to travel by bus, check the schedules and, to ensure a seat, buy your ticket the day before the trip, or at least early in the day of the trip.

By train. There is no passenger train service in Mexico with the exception of the Copper Canyon route (see page 123), serviced by a deluxe service that runs between Los Mochis and Chihuahua (15 hours).

Taxis. Taxis are normally not expensive, but if you are in a place where taxis don't have meters, you should definitely ask the driver how much the ride will cost before starting out. In Mexico City *do not hail a passing taxi on the street.* Several crimes involving taxis have occurred in the green VW-mini taxis. Most hotels have official taxi drivers who are regulated by the union and city. Another "safe" taxi option is to use an authorized, or *sitio*, **taxi base**; hotels and restaurants can call these radio-dispatched taxis for you. Official Radio Taxis, Tel. (55) 5271-9146, (55) 5271-9058, or (55) 5272-6125, are also considered safe. You can hire one of these taxis from your hotel; the driver will frequently act as your personal driver, and escort you through your travels in the city. This is a particularly advisable option at night. The average rate for this service is around 100 pesos per hour.

What's the fare to…?   **¿Cuál es la tarifa a…?**

RELIGION

Mexico is predominantly Roman Catholic. However, there are protestant churches in most cities. Churches in larger cities and resort areas often have Sunday services in English. In major cities Jewish services are held in Spanish and Hebrew. In Mexico City consult the Friday edition of *The News* (English newspaper) for details.

What time is mass/the service?   **¿A qué hora es la misa/el servicio?**

Is it in English?   **¿Es en inglés?**

TELEPHONES

Public phones operated by Telmex are in gray booths marked "Ladatel." They are abundant, and offer the cheapest calling options. They operate with Ladatel debit cards, which can be purchased in drugstores and convenience stores in denominations of 30, 50, and 100 pesos. You can also find coin operated public phones in stores and pharmacies, but less frequently. Usually the first minute of any local call costs 2 pesos. If you are going to use a coin operated phone, make sure that you have plenty of 2 peso coins. If you put a 5 or 10 peso coin in the phone and you don't use up all the time you will not get change.

Long Distance Dialing: within Mexico, dial 01; to call the US or Canada, dial 001. Dial 090 from any phone to make a collect call. As a rule, long distance calls are very expensive. Hotels charge extra for long distance calls and you are better off calling collect. You can also use the services offered by *casetas*. They offer operator placed phone calls and usually also have fax service; some provide Internet connections. While the smaller, more remote towns inside Mexico may only have a caseta and no public phones, these type of services are usually more expensive that the ladatel option.

All over Mexico, dial 040 (information, directory assistance), 060 and 080 (police/emergency), 090 (international operator), and 020 (national operator). Remember that directory assistance will only work if you have the exact name under which a phone is registered; for example, the small hotel you know as El Escondite might be registered under the owner's name and there will be no listing for El Escondite. Mexico is changing its phone system to a standardized seven-digit system. If the number you are dialing is less than seven digits, you'll need to add the last one or two digits from the city's area code to the beginning of the number to complete the local call.

Can you get me this number?	**¿Puede comunicarme con este número?**
Collect (reversed-charge) call	**por cobrar**
Person-to-person (personal) call	**de persona a persona**
I want to send a telegram to...	**Quiero mandar un telegrama a...**

TIME ZONES

Most of Mexico is on Central Standard Time (GMT minus 6 hours). The states of Baja California Sur, Nayarit, Sinaloa, and Sonora are on Mountain Standard Time (GMT minus 7 hours). Baja California Norte is on Pacific Standard Time (GMT minus 8 hours). The country observes Daylight Savings Time.

What time is it?	**¿Qué hora es?**

TIPPING

Wages are low in Mexico and most service-oriented employees count on tips to make up the majority of their income. This is especially true for bellboys and waiters. Bellboys receive 5 to 10 pesos per bag; waiters generally receive 10 to 20 percent of the bill, depending on the level of service; some restaurants include the tip in the bill – especially when serving large parties – so check your bill to make sure. Maids receive between 50 and 100 pesos per week, depending of the service. In Mexico, it is not customary to tip taxi drivers, unless they are hired by the hour, or provide touring or other special services. Keep a supply of coins handy for the inevitable tip.

Keep the change.	**Es para usted.**

TOILETS

In Mexico the toilets may be referred to as *baños, sanitarios, tocadores, escusados,* or *WC*. The doors may be labeled *caballeros* or H (*hombres*) for men, and M (*mujeres*) or *damas* for women. Progress has been made recently in keeping public toilets clean, but always carry tissues with you. Usually you have to pay 1 or 2 pesos to get some toilet paper; and an attendant who hands you towels expects a small tip.

Where are the toilets?	**¿Dónde están los baños?**

TOURIST INFORMATION (*oficinas de turismo*)

The Mexican government maintains many tourist offices abroad; in addition, any Mexican consulate will provide information about travel to Mexico and in many cases contain full-fledged tourist offices (see EMBASSIES AND CONSULATES).

Following is a list of some **Mexican Government Tourism Offices**:

Mexico

UK

- Wakefield House, 41 Trinity Square, London
  EC3N 4DJ;
  Tel. (020) 7488-9392

US

- Toll Free: 1-800-44 MEXICO

- 300 N. Michigan Ave., Chicago, IL 60601;
  Tel. (312) 606-9252

- 1200 N.W. 78th Ave., Suite 203, Miami, FL 33126;
  Tel. (305) 718-4091

- 21 E. 63rd St., 2nd floor, New York, NY 10021;
  Tel. (212) 821-0314

Canada

- 1 Place Ville-Marie, Suite 1931, Montréal, QUEB, H3B
  2C3 Tel. (514) 871-1052

- 2 Bloor St. W., Suite 1502, Toronto, ON, M4W 3E2
  Tel. (416) 925-2753

- 999 W. Hastings, Suite 1610, Vancouver, BC, V6C
  2W2 Tel. (604) 669-2845

You can get a list of the local Tourism Offices in the places you are planing to visit by calling Sectur in Mexico City; Tel. (55) 5250-0123.

The best source of tourist information is INFOTUR a service offered by SECTUR, where they provide bilingual tourist information about attractions, transportation, accommodations, and anything else you might need. The toll-free number inside of Mexico is 800-903-9200; the toll-free number from the US is 800-482-9832. Their number in Mexico City is (55) 5250-0123.

Where is the nearest tourist office? **¿Dónde está la oficina de turismo más cercana?**

WEIGHTS AND MEASURES

Length

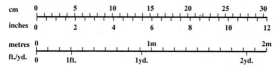

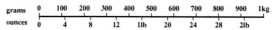

Weight

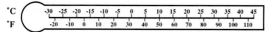

Temperature

YOUTH HOSTELS

Mexico has a network of youth hostels (*albergues de la juventud*) with more than 300 participating hotels and hostels. For information, contact Instituto Mexicano de la Juventud – Turismo Juvenil, Serapio Rendón 76, Col. San Rafael, México, D.F., C.P. 06470.

INDEX